CHRONOLOGY AND HISTORY OF NEPAL

Owing to the antiquity and rarity of this book, certain pages are regrettably absent, and readability is compromised due to the blurring of the original text. If you possess any insights regarding the availability of these missing sections, kindly inform us. Your assistance is crucial in ensuring the completion of this significant work for the benefit of future generations.

CHRONOLOGY AND HISTORY OF NEPAL

[From 600 B.C. to 880 A.D.]

K. P. JAYASWAL

GYAN

Published by

Gyan Publishing House
5, Ansari Road
Daryaganj, New Delhi-110002
Phone: 011-47034999, 9811692060
E-mail: books@gyanbooks.com

Distribution Network
gyanbooks.com
India, USA, Canada, UK, Australia

ISBN: 978-93-7316-636-0 (HB)

First Published, 1937

2nd Impression 2025

Printed at: Gyan Press, Delhi.

CHRONOLOGY AND HISTORY OF NEPAL
Author: K. P. JAYASWAL

Chronology and History of Nepal

[From 600 B.C. to 880 A.D.]

By

K. P. JAYASWAL

1937

TO

RĀHULA SĀṄKṚITYĀYANA

परमार्थशास्त्रकृत्या कुर्वाणः शास्तृकृत्यमिव लोके ।
यो धर्मवता मग्र्यो द्वितीय इव धर्मकीर्तिरिति ॥

PREFACE

Up to this time we had no modern work which dealt with the chronology and history of Nepal from the earliest time to 880 A. D. For the period from 880 A. D. (the foundation of the Nepal Era) to the eighteenth century (when the present dynasty succeeded) the chronology and history have been worked out by Dr. C. Bendall and embodied in the introduction to his Nepal Catalogue of Manuscripts, published by the Royal Asiatic Society of Bengal.

Prof. S. Lévi in Vol. II of his *Le Nepal* has given the abstracts of the Nepal Chronicles which had been brought to notice by the researches of Kirkpatrick, Wright, Bhagwanlal Indraji and Bendall, with the addition of one more edition of the Chronicles (*Vaṁśāvalī*) discovered by him. But Dr. Lévi did not attempt to construct any connected chronology. Further his energy was mostly spent on controverting the dates arrived at for Nepal inscriptions by Bhagwanlal, Bendall and Fleet. Unfortunately Dr. Lévi was not very strong on Indian epigraphy, and he considered Nepal inscriptions to be in eras centuries earlier than those proposed by Dr. Fleet and Dr. Bendall. The inscriptions which had been interpreted by the latter as dated in the Gupta Era (an era starting in 319 A. D.) were placed by Dr. Lévi in the Śaka Era (starting in 78 A. D.). In this great confusion it became necessary to review the whole data and the conclusions thereon by these previous scholars. The reader will find the process and the results in the following pages. Dr. Cecil Bendall has been found to be the most reliable authority on matters epigraphical. His great and long labour on Nepal manuscripts had made him thoroughly familiar with Nepal writings and their times. It was he who first recognised that the years in larger figures in Nepal inscriptions were in the Gupta Era. The result of my enquiry is that Prof. Bendall and Dr. Fleet were right in this respect and Prof. Lévi was mistaken. My conclusion about the other contemporary era of the Nepal inscriptions is that it is not the era of Harsha (beginning in 606 A. D.) as held by Bhagwanlal, Fleet, and Bendall, nor a Tibetan era originating about 593 to 595 A. D. as proposed by Lévi; but a Ṭhākurī Era with its starting point in 595 A. D. instituted by Aṁśuvarman.

The great contribution to the chronology of Nepal by Prof. Lévi is the datum on King Narendradeva, grandson of Aṁśuvarman, from Chinese history, which enables us to correct some important errors in the views of Bhagwanlal and Fleet.

Nepal coins, the Mañjuśrī-Mūlakalpa history, and an astronomical manuscript have been utilized in the present study as additional data. On history—Indian, Nepalese, Tibetan, and Chinese materials have been combined. After the present volume had been printed off fresh evidence has come to light establishing the dominion of the Kushans in Champaran. A hoard of sixty pieces of copper coins of early Kushans was dug out at Raḍhiā, the village which is marked by a pillar of Aśoka. It becomes therefore very probable that the early Kushans ruled also in Nepal, as suggested in this volume. Attention has been drawn to the stone monuments which are in line with Early Gupta Art and which the writer has personally seen and examined.

The Nepal chronicles have misplaced the Kirāta Dynasty—Nepal's first dynasty—and the Gupta Dynasty. But for this misplacement and transposition of certain names in the Lichchhavi Dynasty, the Chronicles are correct. Their dates, however, are hopelessly corrupt, owing, amongst other causes, to the Nepalese writers having mistaken in the inscriptions of Aṁśuvarman (seventh century A. D.) the Samvat (of Aṁśuvarman) for the Samvat Era of 58 B. C.

The period surveyed in this volume—about 600 B. C. to 880 A. D.—covers the period that may conveniently be described as the period of Ancient Nepal.

Buddhism was introduced by the Emperor Aśoka into Nepal amongst a population nearly wholly non-Aryan—the Kirātas. Śaivism, the orthodox caste system, and Aryan population in appreciable numbers and as a dominant factor were introduced by the Lichchhavi dynasty for the first time, from the Muzafferpur district, in the third century of the Christian Era, and the process continued on. Nepal is thus intimately connected with Bihar. But Nepal is so secluded and cut off from Bihar along with the rest of Northern India that the Indian knows more of distant lands than of Nepal which is his ancient colony and which has been a part of his Indian empire for centuries and where one of his most sacred shrines is enthroned. Similarly the history of Nepal which should be a subject of attraction to us has remained almost outside the sphere of Indian enquiry.

It is a hopeful sign that the Government of Nepal has just begun taking interest in their historical remains. They have undertaken excavation at Lumbini—the birth-place of the Buddha. In Nepal many sites invite excavation—e.g. the prominent site of the Kailāsakūṭa Palace. Searches are to be made for early inscriptions. Aśoka must have left some records in the valley, as he has left more than four stūpas. The site of the famous Mānagṛiha is yet to be discovered. Nepal, on the surface, is full of inscriptions, where they number by thousands. As yet no search has been made outside the three capitals or a systematic search even in those capitals. It is hoped that interest in the matter will increase in Nepal and a proper department organized. Documents on stone, metal, palm-leaf and paper of great value to the history of Nepal and of Bhāratavarsha are, we believe, sure to come to light if the matter receives official attention. The last earthquake which destroyed thousands of ancient books should serve as a warning against indifference.

It is hoped that this volume may serve to stimulate interest in Nepal itself in recovering and systematising its history.

I am thankful to Ḥis Highness the Maharaja-Marshal of Nepal for allowing me to visit the valley and to have a firsthand knowledge of many materials and matters discussed in this volume.

K. P. J.

CHRONOLOGY AND HISTORY OF NEPAL
600 B.C. TO 880 A.D.

By K. P. Jayaswal

A

Lichchhavis and Thakuris

[350 A.D. to 880 A.D.]

CHRONOLOGY AND HISTORY OF NEPAL

[600 B.C.—880 A.D.]

A

LICHCHHAVIS AND THAKURIS
350 A.D. to 880 A.D.

I.—THE DATE AND ERA OF AMSUVARMAN

In the Nepal chronology the date of Aṁśuvarman is a pivot, like the date of Chandragupta Maurya, to move up and to move down for several centuries. Aṁśuvarman's date is therefore an important matter.

His date as 635-650 A. D. was postulated by Dr. Bhagwanlal Indraji on the basis of the Harṣha Era, that is, taking the dates in his inscriptions to be in the Harsha Era; and his view was accepted by Dr. Fleet and has been followed subsequently by Indian writers. That view needs reconsideration.

On the date of this king we have the following materials. From Tibetan sources we know that the Tibetan emperor Strong-stan-Gampo whose rule is dated at 629 A. D.[1] (V. Smith, *EH.*, 373, 376 *n.*), married Aṁśuvarman's daughter between 628 and 641.[2] From the account of Yuan Chwang, who began his travels in India in 629 and reached China in 645 (V. Smith, 373, 365), we gather that Aṁśuvarman, a reputed author, had passed away before the Chinese pilgrim left India, that he was '*a recent king*',[3] that is, he had died not long ago. His time is thus fixed as a little before 644 or 645, from the Tibetan and Chinese sources.

Now according to Nepal inscriptions, he was alive in certain years of an unnamed era, in years 34, 39, and 44 noted in the records of his reign (Dr. Fleet, *Gupta Inscriptions*, Introduction, pp. 178-180), and he

[1] According to Chinese History he died in 650 A. D. (JRAS, 1880, 438), and according to Tibetan, in 698 A. D.

[2] According to Waddell and Sarat Chandra Das in 641, and according to de Milloué, between 628 and 631 (V. Smith, p. 376 *n.*). The name of the Nepal king, the father of the Princess, is *go-cha* in Tibetan which has been translated as *Prabhā-varman* (JASB, LIX. 54), and *Jyoti-varman* (Sarat Ch. Das, JASB, L. 200). The reference does not necessarily prove that the marriage took place in the lifetime of Aṁśuvarman.

[3] Beal and Watters, ii, 84, leave no room for doubt on the Chinese text. Bhagwanlal Indraji tried to doubt the translation (*IA.*, XIII. 419), and Fleet totally ignored the evidence of Yuan Chwang. The opinion of the Sinologues is unanimous on the passage that Aṁśuvarman is recorded as a past king by Yuan Chwang (*JA.*, 1894, 58).

must have died in or before the year 48 (Fleet, p. 180) in which year the record of his successor J i s h ṇ u-G u p t a is dated and wherein A ṁ ś u v a r m a n is mentioned as a past sovereign. In any case, A ṁ ś u-v a r m a n's rule, therefore, could not have lasted after the 48th year of this era; and as he died before 645 (Yuan Chwang) the era could not begin after (645-48) 597 A. D. There is, however, yet another reference to A ṁ ś u v a r m a n in the Nepal inscriptions. It is an inscription of Ś i v a d e v a I, the Lichchhavi king, whose feudatory A ṁ ś u v a r m a n had been and who mentions him in an inscription dated in the year 316 of an unnamed era (Fleet, 177-78). This era was taken by Fleet to be the Gupta Era, and it is not possible to take it otherwise owing to the known date of A ṁ ś u v a r m a n from the external sources discussed above. This era beginning as it did 316 years before the time of A ṁ ś u v a r m a n (c. 640) must begin in the first quarter of the 4th century and the only known era which falls to commence about that time is the Gupta Era beginning in 319-320 A. D. The inscription of S a m u d r a G u p t a proves the subordination of Nepal to him. There seems to be no room for any doubt that Nepal adopted the Imperial Gupta Era. In the year 316 (635 A. D., 3rd May) A ṁ ś u v a r m a n according to the inscription is feudatory and adviser (though dominant adviser) of Ś i v a d e v a I. The form "*Mahāsāmanta-Aṁśuvarmmaṇā vijñāpitena mayā*"—proves conclusively the subordinate position of A ṁ ś u v a r m a n. In his own inscriptions up to the year 34, Aṁśuvarman calls himself *Mahāsāmanta*, 'High Feudatory'; and in the year 39 he drops that title and adopts '*Śrī*', 'His Majesty.' Aṁśuvarman to start as king would therefore be dated in or about 635 A. D., not much before, and his reign [as king] will fall between 635 and 645 A. D. (Yuan Chwang)—a period roughly of 10 years at the highest. It follows, then, that his own inscription of the year 39 would be about 635 A. D., that the years 35 to 44 or 45 while Aṁśuvarman was alive would cover his whole reign of 10 years. His reign [as king] is thus to be dated between about 635 A. D. and 645 A. D. And the era of these lower figure years must begin in or before 600 A. D. and not after. It, therefore, cannot be the Harsha Era which began in 606-607 A. D.

The Initial Year of the Era of Aṁśuvarman

There is a definite piece of information in Chinese History of the T'ang Dynasty (chapter 221)[1] giving details of Nepal History from contemporary writings which proves that Aṁśuvarman was dead before the year 643 A. D. In the period 642-647 A. D. when the Imperial Envoy from China—Li Y-piao—was on his way to the court of Harshavardhana, he found on the throne of Nepal 'the king Narendradeva [Na-ling-ti-po].' The father of this king whose name we know from inscriptions to be Udayadeva, eldest son (*Yuvarāja*) of Aṁśuvarman,[2] had been deposed by Naren-

[1] Lévi, *JA.*, 1894, 60, 67; *JA.*, 1900, 304.
[2] *IA.*, IX. 170, insc. of the year 39.

Beginning of line 30 of Thankot Inscription of Mānadeva and Jishṇu Gupta.

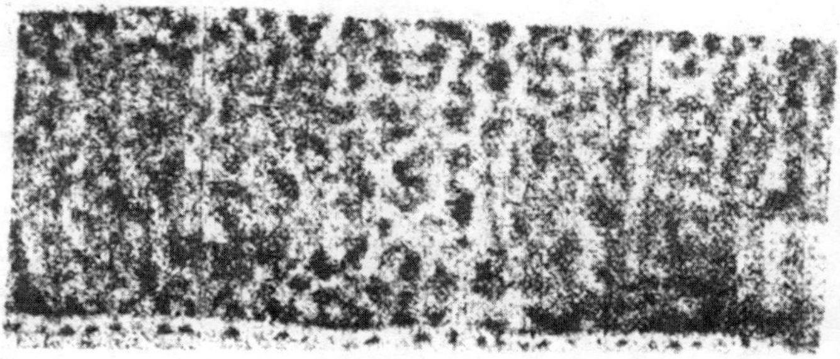

dradeva's uncle, younger brother of his father. Narendradeva was restored to throne by the Tibetan king on the condition that the former became his vassal.[1] Several times two Chinese envoys passed through Nepal between the period 642-647 and 657 A. D. while Narendradeva was ruling. It is an ascertained fact from Chinese history that from 643 A. D. to 657 A. D. Narendradeva was found on the throne.[2] Aṁśuvarman's death therefore is to be dated before 643 and after 635 A. D. when he was alive in the time of Śivadeva I. The period is further narrowed down by the discovery of a further inscription of Śivadeva I, dated 320 published by Professor Lévi in his vol. III on Nepal (p. 79)[3]. This is similar to his other charters mentioning the *Mahāsāmanta* Aṁśuvarman, who had conquered all the enemies. He was thus alive in (320 G. E.) 639 A. D., and his death must fall between 639 A. D. and 643 A. D.

Now can we get at the exact date between these two incontestible dates 639 and 643 A. D.? If my reading of the date as the year 44 in the Thānkot inscription of Jishṇu Gupta (Lévi, iii, plate

[1] The passage has been several times translated by French Sinalogues commencing with St. Julien (*JA*, 1847).

[2] See Lévi, JA, 1894, 55; 1900, 297; *Le Nepal*, i. 155; ii. 164-165; cf. V. Smith, EH, 366, on dates of arrivals of the mission in India.

[3] Discovered by Maharaja Chandra Shamsher Jang at Khopasi (a village to the east of Bhatgaon). Plate XIII of Lévi has the date in perfect and clearest state of preservation, and reads 320, *Chaitra kṛishṇa-pañchamyām*. Unfortunately Prof. Lévi, under his curious idea of Nepal Eras and of Nepal history which minimised the importance of all Gupta connexions in Nepal, read the figure as 520.

XVII), be correct,[1] we can definitely say that Jishṇu Gupta and his puppets, Mānadeva and Dhruvadeva—uncle of Narendradeva and the Lichchhavi succeeding him—ruled for 4 years (yrs. 48[2] and 44 in Jishṇu Gupta's inscriptions), and that the death of Aṁśuvarman is to be dated (643-4) *c.* 639.

Fortunately we have an astronomical datum in an inscription of Aṁśuvarman discovered and published by Dr. Bendall in his *Journey into Nepal* (IA, XV. 338). This is dated in the year 34, in the intercalary month of *Pausha* (*prathama-Pausha śukla-dvitīyāyām*). According to the present system no intercalation is reckoned in Pausha or Mārgaśīrṣa, but that such intercalation was reckoned in the earlier period is confirmed by another inscription noted by Dr. Fleet (*IA*, XV. 338). Now following the system of the old Ārya Siddhānta[3] the month of Pausha will intercalate in the period 600-700 A. D. in four years, namely in 629, 648, 667 and 686 A. D.[4] As 648, 667 and 686 fall in the reigns of Narendradeva and later, we have to select only 629 A. D. as the date when the year 34 of Aṁśuvarman with *prathamu* (1st) Pausha [about November, 23] fell. This will give the initial year of Aṁśuvarman's era to be 595 A. D.[5]

[1] See plate of the beginning of line 30 (enlarged) from Lévi, iii, 104, pl. XVII. Lévi suggested 500, of which there is no trace.

[2] *IA.*, IX. 171.

[3] See Sewell, *Siddhāntas and the Indian Calendar* (p.x).

[4] See Sewell's Tables.

[5] Cf. *JA*, 1894, 62 (Lévi, On the Chronology of Nepal), where he has taken 594, which is an error. His other astronomical facts are also inaccurate. According to the Brahmasid-

His 44th year will thus be 639 A. D.[1] We have therefore to take his death year to be that if the Thankot inscription is dated in the year 44 and his last inscription to be dated in the year 44, not 45 [the reading was doubtful between 44 and 45, Bhagwanlal Indraji, *IA*, IX. 171 *n.* 27; Fleet, *GI*, *I*, 180, *n.* 5]. Otherwise it would fall (in any case) after Chaitra-kṛishṇa-pañchamī, March 639 A. D. and before 643 A. D.

The Chronology of the rule of Aṁśuvarman and Dynastic Revolution on his death

The chronology of the reigns of Aṁśuvarman and Jishṇu Gupta would stand thus.

Aṁśuvarman

595 Beginning of Aṁśuvarman's Era.

625 Aṁśuvarman's Harigaon inscription (Lévi, iii, 85) of year 30, Jyaisṭha 6, fixing maintenance of his commander-in-chief, his coronation horse and elephants, and others.

dhānta (which, Lévi erroneously says, would give the same result) the intercalation of Pausha will take place in 602, 621 and 640 A. D. The Brahma-siddhānta could not have reached Nepal in 602 A. D. or 621 A. D., for it was published and came into use after 628 A. D. (Sewell, p. X). 660 A. D. = 34 of Aṁśuvarman will give us 606 A. D. as the initial year of the era, which we have seen to be impossible. 621 A. D. = 34 of Aṁśuvarman would make him dead in 635 (587 + 48th year when Jishṇu Gupta was ruling), while he was alive up to 639, the 320 year record of Śivadeva.

The astronomical calculations given above have been verified by my friend Dr. Gorakh Prasad, the astronomer of the Allahabad University.

[1] Kirkpatrick's Vaṁśāvalī gives Aṁśuvarman a reign of 42 years.

627 His second Harigaon insc., of year 32, Āshāḍha S. 13, (Lévi, iii. 93), fixing charitable allowances. His Śanga insc. of year 32, Bhādrāpada S. 1, giving a privilege to the village [describing Palace *Kailāśakūta* from which all his charters are issued, as a 'wonder-inspiring' building] Lévi, iii. 99.

629 His insc. of year 34 (Jyaishṭha S.10), IA, IX. 169, on preservation of cocks, pigs, and fishes, etc.

629 His insc. of year 34 (prathama-Pausha S.2), Bendall, p. 74. Grant of fields for repairs of a building.

634 His insc. of year 39, Vaiśākha S.10, order issued as king (*śrī*), for administration in respect of religious (Śaiva) endowments by his sister and her children [IA., IX. 170.]; U d a y a d e v a as *yuvarāja*.

Aṁśuvarman and *Śivadeva* I.

635 Śivadeva I's insc. of year 316 Jyaisṭha S.10 (Bendall, *Journey*, p. 72, IA, XIV. 97) granting privilege to a village on the advice of the *Mahāsāmanta* A ṁ ś u v a r m a n.

639 Śivadeva I's insc. of year 320, Chaitra, Kṛishṇa 5, at Khopasi; privilege to the village on the advice of *Ms.* Aṁśuvarman (Lévi, iii. 79).[1]

639 Vibhuvarman's insc. in the year 44 (or,

[1] There are two more inscriptions of Śivadeva I where *MS.* Aṁśuvarman's advice is cited in the charters, but the dates are gone—IA, IX. 168; Lévi, iii, 62 [Tulachchhitol-Bhatgaon].

45), Jyeshṭha S., when he built a conduit by favour of His Majesty (*Srī*) Aṁśuvarman.

Jishṇu Gupta and *Mānadeva*

639 (?) Thankot inscription of *Srī* Jishṇu Guptadeva, under Baṭṭāraka ['Master'] Srî Mānadeva, '*banner of the family occupying the Lion-Throne*,' of year 44 [?], confirming the grant for a tank made by his own great-grandfather Mānadevagomin. Jishṇu Gupta had his own *Yuvarāja* Vishṇu Gupta, and his dynasty *Soma* [Lévi, iii. 104]

Jishṇu Gupta and *Dhruvadeva Lichchhavi*.

643 Jishṇu Gupta (His Majesty, *Srī*), at Mîna-Nārāyaṇ, in year 48, Kārttika S. 2, makes over to a feudatory a water-course which had been dug out by the "*Mahārājadhirāja Aṁśuvarma-pāda*." The order is passed under the over-lord Dhruvadeva. Jishṇu Gupta claims his sovereignty by hereditary right and popular approval [*IA*., IX. 171].

There is another inscription like the above where the date is mutilated. That also is under Dhruvadeva, the banner of the Lichchhavi dynasty [IA., IX. 173]. The last known inscription [IA, IX. 174] under the prosperous and victorious reign of Srī-Jishṇu-Gupta (Srī-Jishṇu-

Guptasya pravarddhamāna-vijayarājye) has also lost its date.

Narendradeva

643 Narendradeva [grandson of Aṁśuvarman, son of Udayadeva] found by the Chinese already restored on the Nepal throne.

It seems that 643 A. D. was the first year of the restoration of Narendradeva, when Jishṇu-Gupta had been ruling along with Dhruvadeva Lichchhavi whose name we do not find in the Vaṁśāvali [unless it is to be taken as identical with the *Rudradeva*]. The uncle of Narendradeva, therefore must have been Mānadeva who ruled with Jishṇu Gupta before Dhruvadeva who is placed in the Vaṁśāvalis after Udayadeva and is not called *Lichchhavi-kula-ketu* like Dhruvadeva but *siṁhāsanādhyāsi-kula-ketu* in the inscription. It appears that Jishṇu Gupta wanted to legalise his position by setting up a Lichchhavi at Mānagriha in the place of Mānadeva and sought the popular approval as against the claim of Narendradeva.

The Author of the Era 595 A. D.

What does this era which started in 595 A. D. signify?

The Guptas were expelled by Śivadeva I about this time[1]. But then Śivadeva I himself uses the Imperial Gupta era and not a new era. It seems that Aṁśuvarman counted the era from his own coronation as *Mahāsāmanta*,

[1] See separate section on the Guptas of Nepal below.

and it is Aṁśuvarman's own era. He was the founder of a new (the Ṭhākurī) dynasty—an event sufficiently important, especially as it meant the virtual supersession of the ancient and long dynasty of the great Lichchhavis. He counted his original coronation as the reckoning of his new dynasty. That he did not take a formal second abhisheka, at least up to his 34th year, is evident from his inscription where throughout he is styled by the old title *Mahāsāmanta*, although all the paraphernalia and functions mentioned in the inscriptions are fully royal. Probably he was re-anointed in the very last year of his reign as the full title of sovereignty—*Mahārājādhiraja*—does appear on one series of his coins.[1] This was not a posthumous title given by Jishṇu Gupta as supposed by Bhagwan Lal Indraji and Lévi.

A telling argument against the theory of the introduction of the Harsha Era into Nepal is that had it been politically introduced we would have found it also in the inscriptions of Śivadeva I, contemporary of Aṁśuvarman. On the other hand, Śivadeva I and his successors never adopted the era which Aṁśuvarman and his successors used, that is, the era of lower figures—years 30 to 153. It was thus evidently the Ṭhākurī Era, the era of Aṁśuvarman, counted from his coronation as *Mahāsāmanta*.

[1] Cunningham, C. A. I. 117. Lévi, Bhagwanlal Indraji and Fleet have missed this piece of evidence.

A Tibetan Era in Nepal?

Prof. Lévi expounded a theory that Aṁśuvarman's years were in a Tibetan Era (*Le Nepal*, ii, 153-54) which, according to the dates 1203 and 1206 in Dalai Lama's letters of 1789 and 1792 A. D., should have begun in 586 A. D. The Chinese register the foundation of the Tibetan empire in the K'ai-Hoang period which falls between 581 and 601 A. D. Professor Lévi therefore suggests that there was a Tibetan Era which was also the origin of the Bengali Era called "*San.*" Both these theories are untenable.

The Bengal Era though apparently counted from 593 A. D. as its initial year, has really nothing to do with any era starting in 593 A.D. It was invented in the reign of Akbar by taking the years of Hindu eras [Samvat and others] for the year of Akbar's accession and deducting therefrom his accession year in Hijra. His accession occurred in the Hijra year 963; in other systems it corresponded to 1556 A.D. (1556—963 = 593 A.D.)[1]. The origin of the Bengal *San* is thus a new calculation invented in Akbar's reign, and not a Tibetan era. The speculation of Prof. Lévi connecting it with a Tibetan era and assuming a supposed Tibetan conquest of Bengal is a product of unhistorical imagination and complete ignorance of the history of the foundation of the *San-i-Bangálá*, the Fasli year of Bihar and the Vilāyatî year of the Deccan, which all have a common origin, as

[1] See Prinsep's *Essays*, ii. 168; Fleet's *Hindu Chronology* in *Ency. Brit.*, xiii.

fully recorded by Muhammadan historians[1]. Prof. Lévi's method illustrates how a pure philologist makes a poor historian. Prof. Lévi, although he does not say so in clear terms, was swayed [ii. 154] by the name-ending of Tibetan kings *tsan* in attributing a Tibetan origin to the *San* of Bengal, which is not a Tibetan but a Persian word. Tibetans never had any era, that is, a continuous reckoning in their own country. They counted time in cycles and by periods (Prinsep, *Essays*, ii. 160 '*Tibetan Kalendar*'; ii. 289, '*Buddhist Chronology of Tibet*'; Waddel, *Lhasa* (1909), 449, *Tibetan Year-Cycles*). They have a fixed epoch falling in 1025 A.D. which is the year of the introduction into Tibet of the Hindu chronological system called *Kālachakra*. Csoma translated the Tibetan chronology composed in A.D. 1686 (Prinsep, ii. 289) which clearly admits that there was no Tibetan era up to 1686 A.D., that the whole idea of an era was absent in the Tibetan system. For the period before 1025 A.D. Tibet has a fixed epoch of 403 years (Prinsep, ii. 162). Prof. Lévi not finding a possible date in 586 A.D. for Aṁśuvarman's era, proposed that this 403 figure must be a mistake for 430 and deducting from 1025 A.D. reached 595 A.D. and said that that must be the beginning of a Tibetan era which was introduced in Nepal. Now apart from the fact that the whole of the Tibetan chronology negatives the idea of there having been an era in Tibet, Prof. Lévi's proposal to change 403 into 430 is based on no ground. The "epoch of 403 years" is not

[1] Prinsep, ii. 169.

rendered in Tibetan in figures but by a chronogram *mekha-gya-tso* which does not admit of a possible transposition in the process of copying. Further the period "403 years" is too solidly fixed and too well-attested for the interval by noted events to premise a correction (Prinsep, ii. 289).

Now "403 years" before their epoch of 1025 A.D. takes us to 622 A.D. which is really an era, the Hijra era, which Tibet came to know of very early, having come in conflict with the Arabs within the first century of the Hijra—a conflict which continued and lasted for a long time. There is not the least trace in Tibetan books of the establishment of a Tibetan era in 586 A.D., 593 A.D. or 595 A.D.—the dates proposed by Lévi.

It is not possible to hold that the years of Aṁśuvarman are dated in a Tibetan Era. Prof. Lévi says that the adoption of 'the Tibetan Era' signifies the subjugation of Nepal by Tibet. If so, there is no explanation as to why the real king of Nepal, the Lichchhavi Śivadeva (I), contemporary of Aṁśuvarman signing his writ in 316 (G. E.) = 635 A. D. does not adopt the so-called Tibetan Era. He and his successors continue to use another and an older era of three figures (the Gupta Era). If a Tibetan Era was politically introduced in Nepal, it would be expected that the Lichchhavi king in 635 A. D. should have used it as Aṁśuvarman is supposed to have used it. Tibetan influence is assumed on the ground of marriage of the daughter of Aṁśuvarman with the first Tibetan emperor, Srong-tsan-Gampo, whose accession date is definitely 629 A. D. But we find Aṁśuvarman dating his Harigaon inscription in the year 30 (625 A. D.).[1] If it is in a Tibetan Era the introduction of the Era would be even before the accession of Srong-tsan-Gampo! And if we take 'the Tibetan Era' to commence in 586 A.D. the date of Aṁśuvarman's year 30 would be 616, i.e., 13 years before the accession Srong-tsan-Gampo! The whole volume of evidence contradicts the possibility.[2] There is no room for the assumption of the introduction of a Tibetan era before 629 A.D.. Yuan Chwang who passed through the Muzafferpur district in 637 A.D. and took down notes about Nepal in that year knows nothing about any Tibetan suzerainty over Nepal and treats that kingdom as an independent one. In 650 A.D. when Taosuen compiled his *Che-kia-fan-chi*[3] after quoting the description by Yuan Chwang textually he adds "actually the kingdom is under the domination of the Tibetans." The era of Aṁśuvarman's inscriptions which go back to 625 A. D., i.e., some years even before Yuan Chwang's account, could not therefore be dated in a Tibetan Era. Then, if in the year 30 of Aṁśuvarman when he described himself as *Mahāsāmanta*, Nepal had been already conquered by Tibet, how could Aṁśuvarman strike his coins later

[1] Lévi, *Le Nepal*, iii, 85. This inscription was unknown to Bhagwanlal Indraji and Fleet.

[2] See below on the data of the Mañjuśrī History and the Chinese History which definitely date the Tibetan suzerainty after Jishṇu Gupta (successor of Aṁśuvarman) and between 643 A. D. and 647 A. D.

[3] Nanjio, *Catalogue*, (No. 1470; *JA.*, 1894, 60.)

with the full imperial title, that is, the title of an independent sovereign—'*Mahārājādhirāja*' ?[1] Prof. Lévi did not take account of this numismatic evidence at all, otherwise probably he would not have put forward his theory of a Tibetan conquest or suzerainty over Nepal and of introduction of a non-existent Tibetan Era into Nepal.

II.—Constitutional Position of Amsuvarman

The constitutional position of Aṁśuvarman can be gathered from certain Nepal inscriptions and his coins; and that position when ascertained throws some light also on the question of the Era used by him and his successors.

There are nine dated inscriptions on him, giving his titles, which may be compared with the titles on his coins.

[1] Cunningham, CAI, XIII, 5.

Years and Eras	*Record of*	*Titles of Aṁśuvarman*	*Corresponding titles on coins of Aṁśuvarman*
[1] 316 (635 A.D.)	King Śivadeva (*Bhaṭṭāraka mahārāja Śrī Śivadeva*)	"*Mahāsāmanta* (High Feudatory) *Aṁśuvarman*	Nil.
[2] 320 (639 A.D.)	,,	,,	,,
[3] 30 New Era	Aṁśuvarman	"*Śrī mahāsāmanta Aṁśuvarman*"	,,
[4] 32 ,, ,,	,,	,,	,,
[5] 34 ,, ,,	,,	,,	,,
[6] 34 ,, ,,	,,	,,	,,
[7] 39 ,, ,,	,,	"*Śrī-Aṁśuvarman*"	'*Śrī-Aṁśuvarma*' (CAI, Pl. XIII. 4,6)
[8] 45 or 44 New Era	private individual	"*Śrī-Aṁśuvarman*"	,,
[9] 48 ,, ,,	King Jishṇugupta ("*Śrī-Jishṇugupta*")	*Bhaṭṭāraka-mahārājādhirāja Śrī Aṁśuvarman*	"*Mahārājādhirājasya Śryamśoh* (Śrī-Aṁśu's)

[1] Golmāḍhiṭol, Bhatgaon insc. Fleet, G I, *Intro.* 177-8; I. A.; XIV. 97; Dr. Beṅdall was the first to suggest the obvious conclusion from the known date of Aṁśuvarman that the Era must be the Gupta Era.

The inscription is by King Śivadeva I where Aṁśuvarman is adviser and his sister's son Bhogavarman is the *Dūtaka.*

[2] Khopasi, outside the valley, E of Bhatgaon, Lévi, *Le Nepal,* iii. 79 (date misread as "520" for "320").

[3] Lévi, Le Nepal, iii, 95, Pl. XIII; Harigaon insc. I.

[4] Ibid, p. 93, Harigaon.

[5] IA, IX. 169; GI, Intro. 178; Bungmati insc.

[6] GI, Intro. 179.

[7] IA, IX. 170; GI. *I* 179; Devapāṭan insc.

[8] IA, IX 171; G I, *I.* 180; Kathmandu conduit insc.

The above analysis would show

1. that the title *Mahāsāmanta* is given up after the 34th year by Aṁśuvarman, [though the Lichchhavi king still applies it to him up to 639 A.D.];
2. that *Srī* is used as title of full sovereignty, which according to books on constitutional forms and precedents may alone denote '*His Majesty.*' The same *Srī* alone we find on the coins of Māna and Guṇa (CAI, XIII, 1, 2);
3. that the higher—the imperial—title of *mahārājādhirāja* must have been assumed by Aṁśuvarman after or in the year 44/45 and before the year 48, and that he had died before the inscription of Jishṇu Gupta of the year 48;
4. that Aṁśuvarman was never a subordinate of the Tibetan king even up to his death (between years 44 and 48). If Aṁśuvarman had given his daughter to the Tibetan king, so had done the Emperor of China. The alliances prove the importance of Tibet but not suzerainty in either case;
5. that Aṁśuvarman adopted full kingship between the years 34 and 39, and the imperial title after 320 GI [= 639 A. D.]

श्र्यंशुवंम्मंप्रसादेन कारिता सत्प्रणाली विभुवर्म्मणा. There is a doubt as to whether the figure after 40 was 4 or 5. [Nepal Government has extended the parade grounds over this water work; the insc. is lost probably buried under ground.]

[9] IA, XIV. 171; G I, *I*. 180; Lalitapaṭṭana (Chhinnamastikā Temple).

Chaitrakrishna 5[1] in or after and the 44th year;

6. that the era of the 44th year would therefore (639-44) begin in 595 A. D., not later.

If we take into account that he must have been alive in the year of the marriage of his daughter with the Tibetan king (641) and must have died before the year 48—and at least a year before 644 (not later, when Yuan Chwang left the plains of Mid-India), we get the same result, namely, that he died between 639 and 643, and his era was counted from 595 A.D. which he ushered in or about 625 A.D. his 30th year (30th year of his birth or his rule as *Mahāsāmanta*).

If the real position of Aṁśuvarman is realized, it becomes clear that Aṁśuvarman is registering his own regnal years as a subordinate ruler in his inscriptions. The Harigaon record of the year 30, which is the earliest known record of this ruler, shows his exact status. It announces maintenance grants to a number of his officers, his (old?) animals and some idols, after the fashion of 'old kings' पूर्वराजानुवृत्या यथोचितप्रदानानि. The record is in form a royal writ (the donor *samājñāpayati*, 'commands'). The grants are in favour of, amongst others, '*the Commander-in-Chief*' (Mahābalādhyaksha), '*the coronation elephants*,' '*the coronation horse*' (abhisheka-hastinaḥ; abhishekāśvasya), '*the standard-bearer*,' '*the confidential leaders at the time of undertaking an invasion* (or, procession? *Yātrā*). The writ is made known to

[1] Khopasi insc.

the '*Royal Palaces*' (rāja-prasādeshu), and it is laid down in the end that "*future kings*" were not to neglect this favour of their ancestor (न कैश्चिदयम् प्रसादोन्यथा करणीयो भविष्यद्भिरपि भूपतिभिर्गुरुकृतप्रसादानुवर्त्तिभिरेव भाव्यमिति) to emphasize which the Donor says that this he personally commands '*iti svayamājñā*' (as opposed to, through the medium of a *dūtaka*, agent). This of course, amounts to the Donor's own signature. The date he himself puts down along with the subscript *svayam ājñā*, '*saṁvat* 30 *Jyaishṭha śukla shashṭhāyām.*' He is thus talking in terms of a full sovereign, and is directing 'kings' who are to come after him. His title *mahāsāmanta* had ceased to bear its ordinary meaning and had acquired the elevated position of a royal epithet though denoting the origin, like the *Senāpati* with the name of Pushyamitra, 'the sacrificer of two aśvamedhas' (i.e. an emperor: Ayodhyā inscription) where Pushyamitra though already an emperor is still styled as *Senāpati* by his old title. After the style of a full sovereign Aṁśuvarman claims the title of his throne from his respected father (बप्पपादपरिगृहीत:), not from a liege-lord. In other words, any idea of being a feudatory is excluded. And it was to punctuate this that he dates the order in a New Era.

Naturally the old dynasty of the Lichchhavis does not recognise this era of their rival and ex-feudatory and they date as usual in the old Gupta Era. He counts this New or Ṭhākurī Era from his birth or accession as *Mahāsāmanta*.[1]

[1] He is given a reign of 42 years by Kirkpatrick's authority.

The inscription of the year 30 is evidently the first donation on assuming sovereignty. Two years later in another writ of gifts—which is a long list of pious donations (Harigaon Insc. of the year 32: Lévi, iii-92) he says that he was anxious about the happiness of his subjects: कथं प्रजा मे सुखिता भवेद्...In the Bungmatī inscription of again two years later (year 34), he issues a charter to a village community through a dūtaka and refers to himself, addressing his successors, as 'a former king', पूर्वराज-कृतप्रसाद, (IA, IX. 169). He meditated at the feet of his father, that is, as formerly, there is no mention of an overlord. In the Devapāṭan inscription (IA, IX. 170) of the year 39, he is a powerful king, a reformer and has his own *yuvarāja* [*'crown prince'*—Udayadeva] as dūtaka, giving a pious privilege to a foundation of his sister; but he has no title except *Srī*, just as on several issues of his coins.[1] Similarly in the inscription of the year 4[4] which is a private record he is referred to only as *'Srī-Aṁśuvarman.'* These two records mean that *Srī* here stands, as observed above, for 'king' ('His Majesty') and was considered quite sufficient to denote his full sovereignty.

Now let us take the inscription of S i v a d e v a I, the king who refers to A ṁ ś u v a r m a n . In the Bhātgaon writ of the year 316[2] (Gupta Era) of S i v a d e v a, A ṁ ś u v a r m a n is highly praised and described as a great conqueror (प्रख्याताामलविपुलपराक्रमप्रशमितामितविपक्ष-प्रभांवेन), and "to honour

[1] See CAI, XIII; Walsh, JRAS., 1908, p. 669.

[2] See Fleet, G I, p. 178 (*Intro.*) on the date; IA, XIV. 97; Bandall (*Journey.*)

his request" (एतद्गौरवात्) the privilege was granted *to the village. Evidently here* A ṁ ś u v a r m a n is not treated in reality as a subordinate but as an equal sovereign whose request was to be respected and a privilege granted to a village in Ś i v a d e v a's part of Nepal on the recommendation of A ṁ ś u v a r m a n. Ś i v a d e v a's inscription at Buddha Nīlkaṇṭha[1], wherein the date is now missing, shows still more pointedly that more honour and fuller royal honour is accorded to A ṁ ś u v a r m a n than to Ś i v a d e v a himself. A ṁ ś u v a r m a n's great and complete successes in war (यथानेक-पृथुसमरसम्पात-विजयाधिगत-शौर्य्यप्रतापाहृत-सकल शत्रुपक्ष-प्रभावेन,) and his success in kingship (सम्यक् प्रजा-पालन-परिश्रमोपार्जित-शुभ्रयशोभिव्याप्तदिग्मण्डलेन) are so prominently described that it seems certain that A ṁ ś u v a r m a n was treated as king in these inscriptions of Ś i v a d e v a. Although A ṁ ś u v a r m a n was ruling over the 'West', as guessed by Fleet and now confirmed by the Mañjuśrī Imperial History (p. 20), he was practically the real sovereign of Nepal and the position of Ś i v a d e v a had been reduced to that of a nominal, courtesy king of the 'East.'[2] Thus in the Gupta year 316=635 A. D.

[1] IA, IX. 168.

[2] He acts as Dictator in the Eastern part of the kingdom, and as sovereign in the Western part. The grant of privilege to the village of Kurppāsī which is to the E. of Bhatgaon is made 'with the king's approval' by Aṁśuvarman himself, who had dispelled ignorance by the rays of his own virtues, had established welfare by his devotion to Lord Bhava (Śiva), and had uprooted the whole lot of enemies by the strength of his own arms [विदितमस्तु वो यथानेन स्वगुणमणिमयूखालोक-ध्वस्ताज्ञान-

Aṁśuvarman was a full sovereign, and that he had been so for some time. This position he had assumed with his inscription and grants of the year 30, whereby he fixes salaries and allowances for his royal officers. His reference to his coronation horse and his coronation elephants evidently means the animals of the time of his coronation as *mahā-sāmanta*, as there is no indication in the proclamation of any subsequent or recent coronation. His year 30 must be counted from his coronation as mahā-sāmanta. This year 30 being the year of assumption of his ruling powers, must, precede 635 A. D. the date in Śivadeva I's panegyric of Aṁśuvarman.

III.—Confusion In the Chronological Order of Vamsavali Explained.

The Vaṁśāvalīs note in the first place the Mānadeva whom we know to have flourished after Aṁśuvarman, and whose date is known from the inscriptions (GI, 189, I.)[1]; but the Vaṁśāvalīs by a confusion register two Mānadevas *before*

तिमिरेण भगवद्भवपाद-पङ्कजप्रणामानुष्ठानतात्पर्य्योपात्तायतिहितश्रेयसा स्वभुजयुगबलोत्खाताखिलवैरिवर्ग्गेण श्रीमहासामन्तांशुवर्म्मणा]

[1] About one Mānadeva who flourished in the Lichchhavi dynasty we have it on the basis of inscriptions that he was the son of Dharmadeva, grandson of Śaṅkaradeva, and great-grandson of Vṛishadeva, and that he lived *c.* 705-733 A. D. (IA, IX. 163; GI. I, 182; the Changu Narayan Pillar inscription which Mānadeva, himself dated 386 = 705 A. D; IA, IX. 166; the Paśupatinath Temple inscription of the reign of Mānadeva, dated 413 = 732-33 A. D.; IA, IX. 178 : insc. of Jayadeva II of the year 153 at Paśupati Temple mentioning Mānadeva in the genealogy giving his descendants Mahīdeva and Vasantadeva, son and grandson).

Aṁśuvarman. If we look into the list [in IA, XIII 412] we find that Mānadeva is first placed after Dharmadeva, two steps above Vasantadeva, which is his correct position in the inscriptions. Then the name is reported (as No. 25) *once more* after Vasantadeva (no. 23) and Udayadevavarman (no. 24) and one step above Śivadeva (no. 27), predecessor of Aṁśuvarman. We have evidence for the existence of this second Mānadeva. According to the inscription of Jishṇu Gupta at Thankot[1] a Mānadeva who was not a Lichchhavi, ruled as the sovereign (*Bhaṭṭāraka*) of Jishṇu Gupta. According to the Mañjuśrī History, Udayadeva succeeded Aṁśuvarma and was succeeded by Jishṇu Gupta. This is correct, as Udayadeva is *Yuvarāja* of Aṁśuvarman in his inscription. Udayadeva came after Aṁśuvarman, and not before him. After the list—Vṛishadeva to Vasantadeva—which agrees literally with that in the Vaṁśāvalīs, the inscription of Jayadeva II gives, as unconnected with the above in the direct line, (1) Udayadeva, (2) Narendradeva, Narendradeva's son (3) Śivadeva II and the latter's son (4) Jayadeva II (inscription dated 153 = 748 A. D.) Against this the Vaṁśāvalīs have two different data :

[1] Lévi, *Le Nepal*, iii. 104.

(1) *IA*, xiii. 413; *Lévi*, ii. 92, 112	(2) *Kirkpatrick's* Vaṁśāvalī
24. Udayadeva, son of 23.	
25. Mānadeva varman son of 24	
26. Guṇakāmadeva varman, son of 25	
27. Śivadeva varman, son of 26, made Devapāṭana his capital	
28. Narendradeva varman son of 27	
29. Bhīmadevavarman, son of 28	28. Bhīmadevavarman–In his reign the Ahīr Dynasty of the Guptas restored, who were
30. Vishṇudeva varman, son of 29	29. Vishṇu Gupta
31. Viśvadevavarman, son of 30	30. Krishṇa Gupta
[Viśva Gupta—Lévis' *V.*] father-in-law of Aṁśuvarman.	31. Bhūmi Gupta
	New Dynasty
	32. Śivadeva varman *expelled the Guptas and restored the Sūryavaṁśīs*
New Dynasty : Ṭhākurīs	
32. Aṁśuvarman	33. Aṁśuvarman

It is evident that Kirkəpatrick's Vaṁśāvalī here accords with the facts known from inscriptions that Śivadeva [I] who is said to have restored the Sūryavaṁśīs (i.e., the Lichchhavi dynasty, supposed to be a branch of the Ikshvākus—*Sūryavaṁśa*[1]) was followed by Aṁśuvarman. It inserts Vishṇu Gupta (*varmā* of other Vaṁśāvalīs), Krishṇa Gupta, etc. before Śivadeva I, as interlopers. They, as a dynasty, are called "the Guptas," and Ahîrs by

[1] See IA, IX. 178, inscr. of Jayadeva II, where descent is traced from Sūrya.

caste. They were the Later Guptas of Nepal[1] and evidently they claimed suzerainty. They are not in the line of the Lichchhavis. 'Bhīmavarma' is also described as 'Bhīma Gupta' in an earlier list of "the Guptas" wherein Harsha Gupta, Vishṇu Gupta and Jaya Gupta (as the last) also figure (Lévi, ii 73)[2]. These are all Later Guptas. Jaya Gupta is known from his coins of *c.* 600 A. D.[3] Excluding this list of the Gupta interlopers—Bhīma (28 or 29), Vishṇu (30 or 29), Kṛishna and Viśva or Bhūmī (31 or 30)—we get the Vaṁśāvalî list as

1. Udayadeva
2. Mānadeva
3. Guṇakama deva
4. Śivadeva
5. Narendradeva
6. Śivadeva
7. Aṁśuvarman

In the light of the inscriptions, the succession is

Udayadeva
|
Narendradeva
|
Śivadeva (II)

We know the time of Sivadeva II, as he was the father of Jayadeva II who dates his inscription in 153 (748 A. D.). This Śivadeva thus

[1] See below.

[2] The List of the Guptas is given in two places, once in the beginning where Nepal history begins and then under the Lichchhavis, in its proper setting. See below.

[3] CMI, II, 3; CIM, p. 121. See below.

will not be the Śivadeva contemporary of Aṁśuvarman, and has been rightly designated by Fleet as *Śivadeva II.* The Vaṁśāvalīs hence have fallen into a confusion in putting Aṁśuvarman below Śivadeva II owing to the identity of the names of the earlier Śivadeva [I] and the later Śivadeva [II]. The Vaṁśāvalīs have copied two independent lists :

I	II
Udayadeva	Śivadeva I
Narendradeva	Aṁśuvarman
Śivadeva II	

In the second list which is certainly of earlier kings they had two more names above Śivadeva I— namely Mānadeva I and Guṇakāmadeva. That list of earlier kings will thus be :

Mānadeva
Guṇakāmadeva
Śivadeva I
Aṁśuvarman[1]

Was there, then, an earlier Mānadeva, a Mānadeva I, who flourished before Śivadeva I and Aṁśuvarman, and was he succeeded by a Guṇakāmadeva?

According to the inscriptions there is no room for *Guṇakāmadeva* either in the succession later than Śivadeva I, as Mānadeva of Jayadeva's inscription was succeeded by Mahīdeva, his son, who was succeeded by his son Vasanta-

[1] See further discussion below.

deva (also called Vasantasena). There is also no room for a *Guṇakāmadeva* in the other list biginning with Udayadeva which the inscriptions of Jayadeva II and Jishṇu Gupta fix as *Udayadeva—[Mānadeva]—Narendradeva—Śivadeva II—Jayadeva II.* As we shall see below there is no room for a *Guṇakāmadeva* to come in between *Udayadeva* and his son *Narendradeva.* Here coins help us. The *Mānāṅka* and *Guṇāṅka* coins are twins, one follows the other. We have thus the most positive evidence for the existence of Guṇa (kāma) deva.[1] *Mānadeva,* predecessor of *Guṇakāmadeva* has to come earlier than Aṁśuvarman and Śivadeva I.

Let us see if we have any other proof for the existence of a Mānadeva I, that is, a Mānadeva *before* Śivadeva I.

IV.—Manadeva I.

There is good evidence for the existence of an earlier Mānadeva, earlier than Aṁśuvarman, who should be called Mānadeva I. Aṁśuvarman himself mentions a '*Mānagṛiha* gate' to his palace, a god *Māneśvara,* a vihāra *Māna-vihāra.* Śivadeva I issues his charter from *Mānagṛiha.* This would show that there was a Mānadeva before Aṁśuvarman and Śivadeva I.

This is again confirmed by the Mañjuśrī Imperial History (p. 20).[2] It introduces the Lichchhavi line

[1] The style *Mānāṅka* and *Guṇāṅka* has been imitated from the Gupta coin legend *Vikramāṅka* of Chandra Gupta II and other Guptas (*Cf. Garudamadaṅka* and *Parākramāṅka* of Samudra Gupta. Lévi, ii 108.)

[2] See extract below, § VI.

with *Mānavadeva* which has been rightly taken by Lévi to be a mistake for *Mānadeva*. He is placed there definitely before Vṛishadeva and as his predecessor. In the Vaṁśāvalī there is no *Mānavadeva* above Vṛishadeva. Vṛishadeva's time is about 650 A. D. (G. I., p. 189, *Intro.*). The whole succession of 6 generations, from Vṛishadeva to Vasantadeva II, is one from father to son. Vasanta dates his charter in 415[1] (G. E. = 734 A. D.). The inscriptions of Vṛishadeva's great grandson Mānadeva are[2] dated 705-732 A. D. Vṛishadeva came to the throne some time after Sivadeva I. In the genealogy of the Vaṁśāvalīs we have this order:

16 Sivadeva varman (Lévi's *V*, ii. 92).
17 Rudradeva varman
18 Vṛishadeva varman (I. A., XIII. 412).

Here it is evident that the *Sivadeva* I of the inscriptions is the *Siva* (*deva*) *varman* of the Vaṁśāvalīs. *Rudravarman* is omitted in some Vaṁśāvalīs (Lévi, ii. 92), probably he is the same as *Dhruvadeva* of the inscription of Jishṇu Gupta under whom Jishṇu-Gupta grants privileges (I. A., IX. 171).

Exact Date of Mānadeva I

We have now, thanks to the researches of my revered and learned friend the Rājaguru Śrī 6 Pandit Hemarāja Sarmā, C.I.E., a material on the exact date of this Mānadeva, i.e., Mānadeva I has come to light. It is contained in a

[1] See below, the date is 415, not 435 as read by Bhagwanlal Indraji (I.A., IX. 167).

[2] I.A., IX. 163, 166; Fleet, G.I., *I.*, 182.

palm-leaf manuscript which gives his date as equivalent of 576 A. D. The Rājaguru, when he gave me his datum, was of opinion that this Mānadeva for whom he supplied the date from the manuscript was the Mānadeva of the inscription of Changu Nārāyan and that it proved a Mānadeva Era which was the era used by Aṁśuvarman. While I do not accept those views on account of Mānadeva's (III's)[1] dated inscriptions at Changu Nārāyan and Paśupatināth and the other dated inscriptions discussed above and the cross-checks for Aṁśuvarman's years, I gratefully utilize the datum in establishing the time of an earlier Mānadeva, Mānadeva I.

There is a manuscript of a book on Hindu Astronomy called *Sumati-tantra*, which belongs to the State Library of Nepal. The manuscript is in characters what are locally known as the *Gomo lipi*. From its script the date of the palm-leaf manuscript would be the 12th century. I reproduce the pages from a photograph very kindly given to me for that purpose by the learned Rājaguruji. I am told by that scholar that, in the body of the work, in giving examples of calculations the author uses as a pivot the equivalent of the Christian year 576. This would indicate that the author lived very near that date. The author by a chronogram which is contained in the first folio photographed gives the following chronology in verses in Sanskrit of the type of the *Mañjuśrī-mūlakalpa* and other Buddhist works. These verses I

[1] Mānadeva II is the Mānadeva of Jishṇu Gupta's insc.

Leaves of the Sumati-tantra

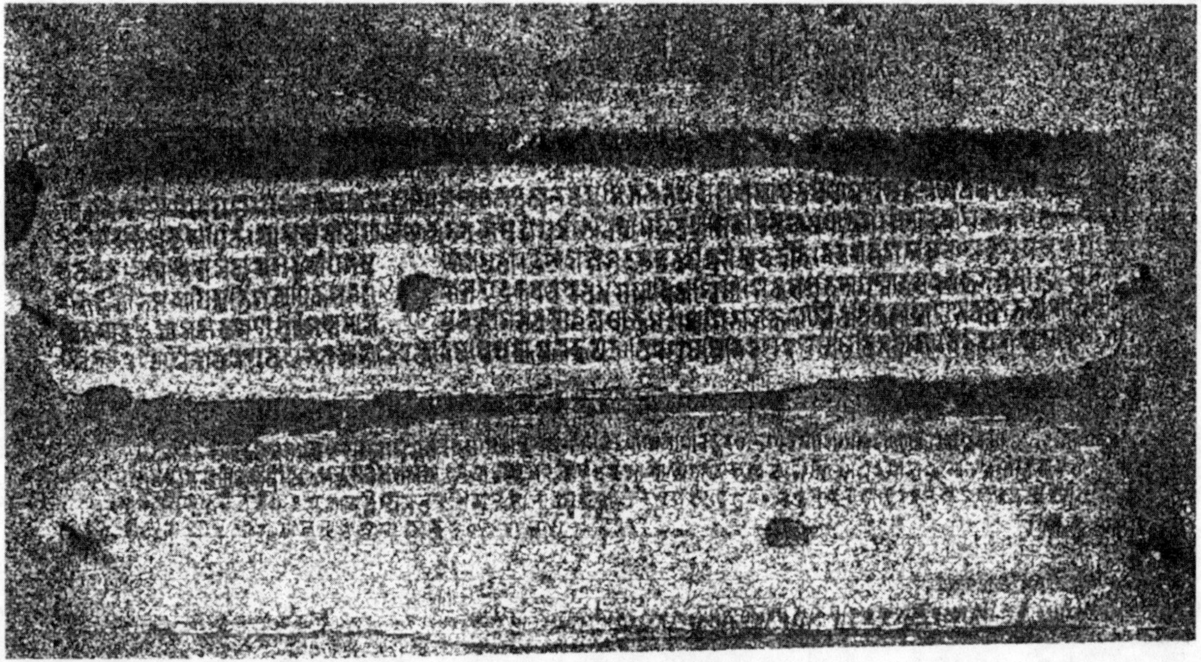

reproduce below from the photograph. Beginning with the K a l i Era, i.e. 3102 B. C., '*the reign of Yudhishṭhira and Duryodhana*,' the author roundly puts 2000 years for the pre-N a n d a period and 800 years more for the pre-C h a n d r a g u p t a (Maurya) period. He gives further 132 years to the Maurya kingdom; then 247 years to that of Ś ū d r a k a, that is, the Sātavāhanas. This brings us to the era of Ś a k a. Then there is an interval of 498 years. On the next page, a subsequent annotator has noted at the end that this interval of 498 brings the chronology to the reign of M ā n a d e v a, and the kingdom of Mānadeva is brought down by 304 years i.e., down to the Nepal Era. The initial year of the Nepal Era falls in 879-880 A. D. (the year beginning on the 1st Kārttika Sudi—*G.I.*, Intro. 74). 498 years before it will take us to 576 A. D. as the year of Mānadeva I. Knowing as we do the initial year of Śaka—78 A.D., 498 years after it brings us to the same year (78+ 498 =) 576 A. D. These three dates are the only definite dates which the Nepal astronomers—the author of the *Sumati-tantra* (the '*Sumati system*') and the annotator—knew : the Śaka era, and the initial year of Mānadeva I, and the Nepal Era. The annotator could calculate it from both the eras if he knew the correct interval from either. In the 12th century when the book was copied it is very likely that the astronomers of Nepal knew the correct date of M ā n a d e v a I. I have myself seen a number of hand-written books in possession of the Rājaguru which are note-books of the past centuries of Nepal astronomers, recording chief contemporary events, made and left as heirlooms, for future use by their successors. Documents four and three hundred years old both on paper and palm-leafs are commonplace in Nepal families even today. I found one family possessing two hundred palm-leaf sale-deeds of the time of the Malla dynasty. They bear the original royal seals intact.[1] I saw a whole book—a long paper-roll folded as pages—which was originally written in 721 N.E = 1601 A. D. by the builder of the Mahābodhi temple at Bhatgaon, noting in full the description of the process of building the temple as a guide for future repairs. The book is being used today for repairing the damages caused by the earthquake of 1934. The habit of valuing old records and the climate are both in favour of this fortunate circumstance. It is thus reasonable to suppose that the annotator of the *Sumati-tantra* actually had reliable records before him for the date of Mānadeva I.

The chronology before the Śaka Era is not reliable, but its dates about Chandragupta Maurya and the dynasty of Śūdraka (Simuka = Śūdraka Sātavāhana) are interesting, being very near the true marks.

[1] Three of these I have brought and deposited at the Patna Museum. We have discovered in British India thousands of sealings of Hindu times but not a single example of a document with a sealing attached. Now we can see from the Nepal documents, discovered for the first time, how the seals were actually attached to documents by the royal office. They were clay (unbaked) sealings of a very cementing composition. A strip of palm-leaf tied the document after the fashion of inserting strips of leather in our leather shoes and then the joint was sealed. I hope to publish these examples in this Journal.

The text is as follows :—

.. ..

L2.)·······यातास्तथा युगाना(—)वा कृत मन्ता(?)थ द्वापरं।
भविष्यं संप्रवक्ष्यामि कालिकं वा यथाक्रमं।
जातो दुर्योधनो राजा कलि (. .) (L3.) प्रवर्त्तते।
युधिष्ठिरो महाराजो दुर्योधनस्तथाऽपि वा।
उभौ राजौ सहस्रे द्वे वर्षन्तु सम्प्रवर्त्तति।
नन्दराज्यं शताष्टं वा श्चन्द्रगुप्तस्ततो पर (म्)।
L4.)राज्यङ्करोति तेनापि द्वात्रिंशच्चाधिकं शतम्।
राजा शूद्रकदेवश्च वर्षसप्ताब्धिचाश्विनौ।
शकराजा ततो पश्चाद्वसुरन्ध्रकृतन्तथा।
इत्येते (भा)(L5.)षितं मह्यं ज्ञेया राजा क्रमेणतु

....

[*Note*]·······युधिष्ठिर दुर्योधन उभौ राज्याब्द २०००[,]नन्द राज्याब्द ८००[,]चन्द्रगुप्त राज्याब्द १३२[,]शूद्रकदेव राज्याब्द······शक राज्याब्द ४९८[,]मानदेवस्य राज्याब्द ३०४[.] शुभम्

The translation is :

(Line 3) Duryodhana was born in Kali.

Yudhishṭhira and Duryodhana : "*the two kings last for* 2000 *years.*"

"*Nanda's kingdom* (*rājya*) *lasts for* 800 *years.*"

"*Chandragupta is after that. He also rules for* 132 *years.*"

"*The king Śūdraka for* 7, 4 (*abdhi*) and 2 (*aśvinau*) (i.e. for 247) *years.*

"*After that, similarly, king Śaka*, 8, 9, 4 (that is, for 498) *years.*"

For the *Nanda-rājya*, it gives the year (3102 B. C.—2000 =) 1102 B. C., and for the beginning of the Maurya kingdom it gives (1102-800 =) 302 B. C., for the Sātavāhana kingdom, (302-132 =) 170 B. C., and for the Śaka kingdom, (247-170 =) 77 A. D.

(elapsed) i.e. 78 A. D. The dates for the commencement of the Maurya kingdom and the Sātavāhana kingdom are short by about 22 years each. The year for the commencement of the Nanda-Rājya is hopelessly wide off the mark.

It is clear that the author of the chronology took chief re'gns as land-marks, and not always eras. There were Yudhishṭhira, Nanda, and Śaka Eras, but there was no Chandragupta Era, there was no Sūdraka Era. There is no trace of an Era of Mānadeva I, for we find Śivadeva I the Lichchhavi using not a recent era but the Gupta Era in 635 A. D. Nor could the Era of Aṁśuvarman be a Mānadeva Era, commencing from 576 A. D., for in that case Aṁśuvarman must be dead in (576 + 48 =) 624 A. D. but he was alive in 635 A. D. (the date of Śivadeva I's inscription and later (see above). Evidently the author was a contemporary of Mānadeva I and used his coronation year for his calculations.

We are on firm ground in taking 576 A. D. as the first year of Mānadeva I, as it receives corroboration not only from the script on the *Mānāṅka* coin, which Dr. V. Smith assigned to the 6th century A.D. (C. I. M., p. 281) but also from the dates of Vṛishadeva and Śivadeva I, before whom Mānadeva I must come.

Another copy of the *Sumati-tantra* is in the British Museum Library. It is a palm leaf manuscript dated in Nepal Era, 476 (1356 A. D.). The copy is much later than the one to which reference is made above. With its help we have to read *Kali-sandhyam* in our line 2. It reads *śatāshṭañcha* against *śatāshṭam vā* (line 3) of my manuscript[1]. While these are minor improvements, the two important figures for *Śūdraka* and Śaka-rājā are clearly wrong in the British Museum copy which reads राजा शूद्रक देवश्च वर्षं सप्ता द्वि चाश्विनौ

in place of „ „ „ „ ब्धि „

and शक राजा ततो पश्चाद्वसु चन्द्र कृतन्तथा,

in place of „ „ „ „ रन्ध्र „

These two figures would date the Saka era twenty years earlier than its true date which the other manuscript gives correctly. The interval between Śaka and Mānadeva, read by it as of 418 years as against 498, is proved to be wrong by the next interval of 304 years which brings the chronology to 880 A.D., the beginning of the Nepal Era. The British Museum MS. will put Mānadeva at 496 A. D. (418—78 A. D.) or at 476 A. D. taking its other mistake (of 20 years placing Śaka at 58 A. D.). The last interval of 304 will then bring the chronology to 800 A. D. or 780 A. D., that is, there will be a discrepancy of 80 or 100 years. The two mistakes in the British Museum copy are produced by simple misreadings in Nepal scripts: *dvi* (द्वि) for *bdhi* (ब्धि) and *chandra* (चन्द्र) for *randhra* (रन्ध्र).

The British Museum copy has a prose line after the text ending with *kramena tu* which is not to be found in the older manuscript—

सेषा युताश्च कृत अम्बराग्नि ३०४ श्रीमानदेवाब्द —प्रयुज्यमाना एतानि पिण्डकलिवर्षमाहुः ॥

[1] *Catalogue of the Sanskrit Manuscripts in the British Museum* by Cecil Bendall, (1902), pp. 193-94, 467. No. 3564. Although the opening passage quoted gives the name as *Sumati-tantra*, it is wrongly catalogued as *Sumata*.

"The rest (of the kings), added together, employ the year (era ?) of Mānadeva for 304 (years)—these years are called the collective Kali reckoning."

Dr. Bendall, not following the chronology of the text, added the figure 418 (after Saka) to 304 and obtained 800 A. D. as the date of Mānadeva, while Mānadeva begins, according to the system followed in the chronology, when the 498 or 418 period after Saka ends.

V.—Lichchhavi Kings

The complete list of the Lichchhavi kings as in the Vaṁśāvalīs may be divided in three parts.

I

Serial numbers according to the order in the Vaṁśāvalīs. (I.A., XIII. 412; Lévi, ii. 91-92, 122).	Names noted in Jayadeva II's inscription.	And other inscriptions.
[1]1.	Bhūmivarman (capital at Bāṇeśvara).	Names Nos. 1,2, 4-16 purposely omitted in Jayadeva II's insc. (I.A., IX. 178).

[1] Kirkpatrick's authority gives five more names to this dynasty which is unanimously called Sūrya-Vaṁśī. These five names are given separately by the Vaṁśāvalīs, other than Kirkpatrick's, under Somavaṁśī Dynasty. This is a wrong division, as the Vaṁśāvalīs themselves note the connexion between Bhāskaravarman (no. 5 and the last) of the so called *Soma vaṁśa* and Bhūmivarman (no. 1 of the Sūryavaṁśa) as that of adoptive father and son. How could then the Vaṁśa change ?

2.	Chandravarman	
3.	*Jayadeva*[1] I	Jayadeva I according to J.II's insc. he was founder of the Nepal dynasty. An earlier king *Supushpa* is noted as having flourished at Pushpapura; "omitting 23 Kings" there comes Jayadeva I '*the victorious*.' Then *omitting in the interval eleven kings*, there comes the 12th according to the inscription but the 18th V ṛ i s h a d e v a, according to the Vaṁśāvalīs
4.	Varsha-varman [Vṛishavarman I K.]	
5.	Sarva-varman	
6.	Pṛithvi-varman	
7.	Jyeshṭha-varman	
8.	Hari-varman	
9.	Kuvera-varman	
10.	Siddhi-varman	
11.	Haridatta (built 4 Nārāyana Temples including Changu Narayan and Nīlakaṇṭha Jalaśayana[2] Temples)	
12.	Vasudatta	
13.	Śrīpati	
14.	Śivavṛiddhi-(varman)	Śivadeva I[3] (I. A., IX.)
15.	*Vasantadeva I*	Dhruvadeva
16.	Śivadeva I	I.A., IX. 173

[1] '*Jayavarmā*' in the Vaṁśāvalīs which have throughout for nos. 1 to 14 name-ending *varman*. Kirkpatrick's Vaṁśāvalī has *deva* from no. 15 onwards, while other copies occasionally add *varman* to *deva*. Inscriptions have always *deva*. I have followed generally K.'s list for name-forms. His copy is the oldest and more valuable.

[2] *Jalaśayana*, a colossal, lying figure of Vishṇu, is a magnificent stone image in Gupta style.

[3] I.A., XIV. 97 (Bendall); I.A., IX. 168 (Bhagwanlal Indraji); Lévi, iii, 61, *Dūtaka*-Bhogavarmagomin, mentioning the request of A ṁ ś u v a r m a n; the date is wholly gone. Prof. Lévi insists on reading all figures in Ś i v a d e v a ' s records as 500 (+) instead of 300 (+) as read by Bhagwanlal Indraji, Bendall and Fleet. The last record has no trace of the date, yet he sees here also 500. The reading 300 (+) is corroborated by the figures in records of subsequent kings—of Mānadeva II, Vasantasena, etc. (386, 413, 435) (G.I., *I.* 180) and by the new, Khopasi, insc. of Ś i v a d e v a I published by Lévi himself (iii. 79) where his plate (XII) reads clearly 300 (+20). This also mentions A ṁ ś u v a r m a n.

6

II

17.	Rudradeva[1] (given by some and omitted by K.)		
18.	Vṛishadeva II (a noted Buddhist pious founder)	(12) Vṛishadeva	Vṛishadeva I.A., IX. 163
19.	Śaṅkaradeva [Revival of Śaivism (erected a trident at Paśupati)[2]	(13) Śaṅkaradeva	Śaṅkaradeva
20.	Dharmadeva	(14) Dharmadeva	Dharmadeva
21.	Mānadeva	(15) Mānadeva	Mānadeva
22.	Mahīdeva	(16) Mahīdeva	
23.	Vasantadeva II	(17) Vasantadeva	Vasantasena

Jayadeva II omits the first two names of the list and he counts 17 as against (23-2) 20 successions[3] down to Vasantadeva II. There are therefore 3 extra names in the V. list, or, rather 5 if we transpose Mānadeva and Guṇakāmadeva from the part III (see below, and § IV above). These extra names fall between no. 3 Jayadeva I, and no. 18 Vṛishadeva, the later names being confirmed by inscriptions. And as the existence of nos. 16 and 17 (Dhruvadeva) is certain from contemporary records, the excess has to be adjusted between no. 3 and no. 15 taking account of Mānadeva I

[1] Lévi, ii. 92, 95-96, regards him as identical with Śivadeva and thinks that the name is transposed from the Malla list.

[2] The trident is still existing. The big metal Nandi, attributed to him by some Vaṁśāvalīs to his son, is also still there.

[3] The Vaṁśāvalīs regard the successions as from father to son in each case, which is to be ignored unless confirmed by the evidence of inscriptions or contemporary writers.

and Guṇakāmadeva. According to the inscription of Jayadeva II and the evidence on Mānadeva I and Guṇakāmadeva the kings have to be numbered thus:

1. Jayadeva I (*c.* 350 A.D.)
2-7. Six kings (which should include Haridatta, see below), against 11 of the Vaṁśāvalīs
8. Vasantadeva I
9. Mānadeva I, 576 A.D. (see § IV)
10. Guṇakāmadeva
11. Śivadeva I—635-639 A.D. (Khopasi insc. 320 G. E.)
11*a*. Dhruvadeva *c.* 643 A.D. (Jishṇu Gupta's insc. of yr. 48) not taken into account probably owing to his being an unlawful successor
12. Vṛishadeva
13. Śaṅkaradeva
14. Dharmadeva, 705 A.D.
15. Mānadeva II, 705, 732 A.D.
16. Mahīdeva
17. Vasantadeva II, 735 A.D. [G.E. 415[1]; dead in 732 A.D., yr. 153, *āsit*]

Out of Nos. 4 to 14 of the Vaṁśāvalīs (wherein the extra five names must fall), Haridatta, no. 11, must be a correct name. Vaishṇavism was introduced into his reign and his Vaishṇava monuments can still be identified. Although the present temple of Changu Nārāyan is much later but that the shrine must go back to about his time is proved by the inscription

[1] The reading of the figure is 415, not 435; cf. plate 2 in I.A., IX, with plate 3.

of Mānadeva II on the dhvaja standard at Chaṅgu-nārāyan, which is in early Gupta style[1], and, by the grand J a l a ś a y a n a figure at Nīlakaṇṭha which is again typically Guptan, and which is mentioned by Aṁśuvarman in his Harigaon inscription of year 32.[2] As to the other names we have at present no means to check and to accept or reject. But there should be a presumption of correctness in their favour, as a very high percentage of data in the lists of the Vaṁśāvalīs is proved to be correct. The number of 11 princes of the list as against 6 out of the unnamed 11 of the inscription of Jayadeva II means that between Jaya-deva I and Vasantadeva I (no. 1 to 8 of my list above) the first eight kings, there were two contemporary lines ruling as in the later period. This system of double rule seems to have been borrowed from the home constitution of the Lichchhavis of Vaiśālī.

The Vaṁśāvalīs after their no. 23 present a great confusion, which has been already solved with the help of the inscriptions to some extent, and the solution can be carried further with the help of new data.

III

This portion of the so-called Lichchhavi list I am marking as part III. The list is a mixture of the names of the EARLY ṬHĀKURĪ Dynasty with some names of the Lichchhavis transposed and

[1] It is also mentioned by Aṁśuvarman at Harigaon (Lévi, iii. 94).

[2] Lines 14-15 (Lévi, iii. 95).

names of one more dynasty, 'Gupta-Ahīr', that is, the Later Guptas of Nepal (see § 6—7).

Vaṁśāvalī list

Kirkpatrick, 260; Bhagwanlal Indraji, 13I.A. 413. Wright, 124—130; Lévi, ii. 92, 122.

24. Udayadeva
25. Mānadeva
26. Guṇakāmdeva
27. *Śivadeva* ('transferred the seat of government to Devapāṭana')
28. Narendradeva
29. Bhīmadeva varman

According to K's V., Gupta Dynasty of Ahīr caste:

30. Vishṇu gupta (K) (Vishṇudeva varman—others)
31. Viśva Gupta (Viśvavarman—others) gave his daughter in marriage to *Aṁśuvarman*, founder of the Ṭhākurī Dynasty.
K's *Vaṁ*. gives after no. 30—
31. Kishnu Gupta
32. Bhūmi Gupta

33. Śivadeva expelled the Guptas; and restored the Sūryavaṁśī (the Lichchhavi) dynasty (K.)

A ṁ ś u v a r m a n [595—539 + (?) A.D.]

Against this we have the following succession from inscriptions (I.A., IX. 170, 174, 178).

[*Vaṁ.*] *Inscriptions*

[24.] Udayadeva, (*Yuvarāja* in yr. 39) deposed by his younger brother (Chinese History).

[25.] Mānadeva (III) (evidently brother of 24, as 27 Narendradeva, restored by Tibetans, was son of 24).

[28.] Narendradeva [ruling from 634 to 657, according to Chinese (Thang) History].

[29.] *Sivadeva II.*, yr. 119.

Jayadeva II, yr. 153 (Vaṁśāvalīs omit him).

The order in V. between 27 and 28 is transposed, and Guṇakāmadeva is brought down from below Mānadeva I (above Śivadeva I) to be placed below no. 25 Mānadeva III, above Śivadeva II.

These are all later than Aṁśuvarman whose last date in inscriptions in the year 44 (or 45). These are all, as we shall see presently, Ṭhākurī names. Jayadeva II, son of Narendradeva, is neither in the Ṭhākurī list nor the Lichchhavi list of the Vaṁśāvalīs. The reason for this is explained in the Ṭhākurī section. Aṁśuvarman has been placed in the V. list after Śivadeva II who lived about the year 119. There is fortunately only one Aṁśuvarman and we easily detect the mistake. There have been two mistakes. No. 25 and 26 have been removed from their place above Śivadeva I to be placed, above Śivadeva II. Aṁśuvarman's history is transferred to the time of Śivadeva II from Śivadeva I which is evident from K.'s copy. In the eighteenth century, Vaṁśāvalī copies still preserved the close association of the history of Śivadeva I and Aṁśuvarman, and Kirkpatrick's copy for that reason introduced even a third Sivadeva (no. 33). But later editions noting (correctly) only two Śivadevas, cut Aṁśuvarman off from Śivadeva altogether owing to their insertion of several names (nos. 30, 31,

32) above Aṁśuvarman's, which fortunatly for us Kirkpatrick's copy specially notes as names of an intervening family who were defeated by Sivadeva I. That Sivadeva II can not be a contemporary of Aṁśuvarman is clear from the dated inscription of Śivadeva II (of the year 119) and from the date of his father known to us from Chinese History based on contemporary writings.

Now as to the "Guptas" who were expelled by Śivadeva I according to Kirkpatrick's Vaṁśāvalī, is there any trace of theirs in the inscriptions?

These Guptas seem to be the ancestors of Jishṇu Gupta whose inscriptions we have as nos. 9, 10, and 11 of Bhagwanlal Indraji (I.A., IX. 171, 173). A new inscription of his is published by Lévi (*Nepal*, iii. 102, pl. XVII; Thankot inscription). The last one bears the date (saṁvat) 44(40 + 4)[1] the figure for 40 is distinct (line 30th). The writ was dated while *Bhaṭṭāraka* (Sovereign) Srī Mānadeva [II] was '*the banner of the enthroned family*' at Mānagṛiha; it was issued by Sri Jishṇu Gupta Deva from Kailāsakūṭabhavana[2].

[1] It is difficult to imagine how could Prof. Lévi read 500! I am giving an enlarged copy of the portion (beginning of line 30) from his plate. See my plate VII.

[2] *Kailāsakūṭa* was the seat of the Dictator, and *Mānagriha* was the seat of the nominal king. Aṁśuvarman built this famous Palace Kailāsakūṭa, of which he is very proud in his Sanga insc. (Lévi, iii 99). His family after him ruled from it (we have reference to it in inscriptions down to the time of Śivadeva II (9I.A. 174), while the Lichchhavis lived at their Palace Mānagṛiha, (G.I, *I*, 188-189) built evidently by Mānadeva I (576 A.D.—) as Aṁśuvarman named one of the gates of his own palace after *Mānagriha*. In this inscription we have the novel position that Mānadeva (II), a younger son of

It confirmed a donation, the document of which had been lost; it was orginally made by the great grandfather (*prapitāmaha*) of Jishṇu Gupta, whose name was Mānagupta Gomin. It refers to certain taxes payable in kārshāpaṇas and one of the taxes was *Malla-kara*. This had been evidently imposed to meet the incursions of the Mallas which were put an end to by Mānadeva III who in his Chaṅgu Nārāyan inscription says that he crossed the Gaṇḍakī with his cavalry and elephants and conquerred the Malla towns (Lévi, iii, 14)[1].

Mānagupta Gomin must have been a subordinate ruler having Thankot, i.e. the beginning of the valley, under his jurisdiction. The title *gomin* meant in Gupta times '*honourable*'

Aṁśuvarman and a younger brother of Udayadeva (§ IX) is installed by Jishṇu Gupta (who calls himself 'king,' '*deva*') at Mānagṛiha and he himself takes his residence at Kailāsakūṭa. This shows that Kailāsakūṭa was the official seat of the official Dictator.

For the time being by the above arrangement the Lichchhavi Dynasty was wholly dispossessed on the death of Aṁśuvarman. But this was only for a year or so, for soon after we find the Lichchhavi king Dhruvadeva at Mānagṛiha once more during the Dictatorship of Jishṇu Gupta. Jishṇu Gupta in both cases was the real ruler, and although the Vaṁśāvalīs ignore him, he is noted as king by the Mañjuśrī History (§ VI).

The family emblem of the Ṭhākurīs was Nandi seated on Kailāsakūṭa—see plate 12, I.A, IX.

The latest mention of Mānagṛiha is found in the Isapaligaon inscription of the year 489—808 A.D. published by Lévi in his volume iii, pl. VIII, p. 59. [This inscription, where the writing is distinctly much advanced, most effectively destroys the theory of Lévi to read the date figures in Śivadeva I's inscriptions as 500 + , instead of 300 + as read by Bhagwanlal and confirmed by Fleet and Bendall].

[1] This text (lines 22-25) was recovered from the buried portion of the pillar, not available to Bhagwanlal Indraji.

and is used as a name-ending in respectable names—e.g. *Chandra gomin*, the Grammarian, *Bhogavarmagomin* in Aṁśuvarman's inscription. Māna Gupta is not described as a king, or given any title. The two generations before Jishṇu Gupta would cover the two names Vishṇu Gupta (no. 30) and Viśva Gupta (31), the latter being the father-in-law of Aṁśuvarman, whose place in K.'s Vaṁs. is given to Bhūmi-Gupta (32). Viśva Gupta and Bhūmi-Gupta were the last of the Nepal Guptas, and Śivadeva I defeated them and "restored" the Lichchhavi dynasty. Evidently the Lichchhavi dynasty had suffered an eclipse at the hands of these 'the Ahīr' Guptas, probably in the time of or just after Guṇakāmadeva I, as no coin is struck by Śivadeva I.

Jishṇu Gupta described himself (under Mānadeva II) as an ornament of the moon dynasty (*Somānvaya-bhūshaṇa*) and as having succeeded to a hereditary throne. Kirkpatrick's authority relates that these 'Aheer' Guptas were a branch of the Goalā Guptas. But the Nepal Guptas claimed to be Kshatriyas of the Moon Dynasty. The Moon Standard on the coins of the Imperial Guptas implies the same claim. Jishṇu Gupta is not mentioned in the Vaṁśāvalīs or the inscriptions of the Lichchhavis or the Ṭhākurīs. Officially he was the Dictator; his *Yuvarāja* Vishṇu Gupta did not come to the throne. The way he refers to Aṁśuvarman [*Śrī Aṁśuvarmapādaiḥ*, IA, IX. 172] shows that he was related to him, evidently through the latter's marriage

7

with Viśva Gupta's daughter. Jishṇu-Gupta seems to have been the son of Viśva Gupta. He to make room for himself in the Lichchhavi constitution—for the position which had been occupied by Aṁśuvarman, and which lasted up to the year 320 (639 A.D.) when Śivadeva I inscribed his last known order—seems to have removed Mānadeva II, the usurper, the second son of Aṁśuvarman, and set up Dhruvadeva Lichchhavi in the brief period of his total dictatorship of 3 or 4 years. In the inscription under the sovereignty of Dhruvadeva (IA, IX. 171) he protests that he belongs to a pious family (*puṇyānvaya*) and that his rule is supported by the Pauras (*paurā śritaśāsana*), which probably implies commotion about the year 48 (643 A.D.) when very soon he was going to be dispossessed by Narendradeva, son of Udayadeva. Both he and Dhruvadeva are ignored in the Vaṁśāvalīs and Ṭhākurī inscriptions, as usurpers. Except for the Mañjuśrī History[1] we have had no reference to him in literature. He imitates the coins of Aṁśuvarman.

Dhruvadeva did not belong to the direct Lichchhavi line and his selection as king must have been at the cost of Vṛishadeva. There is no coin of Dhruvadeva; the right of coinage was exercised by JishṇuGupta.

We can date the order of succession of this part thus, taking Udayadeva the *Yuvarāja* as the eldest son of Aṁśuvarman:

[1] See below, § VI.

Lichchhavis	*Guptas*	*Ṭhākurīs*
Dhruvadeva (643 A.D.)[1]	JishṇuGupta	Udayadeva
Vṛishadeva	with his Yuvarāja VishṇuGupta (yr. 48)	Mānadeva II (between yrs. 44 and 48)
Śaṅkaradeva		
Dharmadeva [upto 705, defeated and killed the Tibetan in 705 A.D., (JRAS, 1880, 438) and set up four Pillars of Victory]		
Mānadeva III, 386 GE. (=705-732)		Narendradeva (643-657)[1]
Mahīdeva (after 413GE. = 732 A.D.)		Śivadeva II, yr. 119 (714 A.D.)[2]
Vasantadeva 415 GE. (=734 A.D.)		Jayadeva II, yr. 153 (748 A.D.)

J a y a d e v a II after detailing the Lichchhavi family from Vṛishadeva to Vasantadeva II gives '*within*' (*asya antare*) the period of this dynasty (vaṁśasya) his own genealogy contemporary with those Lichchhavi kings. He naturally omitted the interlopers J i s h ṇ u-G u p t a, M ā n a d e v a III, and D h r u v a d e v a. Owing to D h r u v a d e v a intervening between

[1] Lévi, ii, 164. Narendradeva, son of Udayadeva, succeeded with the help of the Tibetans and was ruling in 643, while the year (48) in which the reign of Dhruvadeva is dated, also corresponds to 643 A.D.

[2] His reign (714 A.D.) falling 57 years after his father's, he must have been a baby on the death of his father.

Śivadeva I and Vṛishadeva, the Lichchhavi kings are taken up from Vṛishadeva, and after finishing that line the contemporaries—the Ṭhākurīs—are given, which necessitates the omission of Aṁśuvarman. The descendants of Aṁśuvarman probably imply a claim to be Lichchhavis by the inscription of Jayadeva II. This is explained by the statement in some Vaṁśāvalīs (cited in Landon's *Nepal*, ii. 315) that Aṁśuvarman had been adopted as son by Śivadeva I. This seems to explain the anomalous position of the Ṭhākurīs both in the inscription of Jayadeva II (IA, IX. 178) and the Vaṁśāvalī list. This also explains the revolutions in the time of JishṇuGupta, Mānadeva II and Dhruvadeva.

When Jayadeva II wrote his inscription in the year 153=748 A.D. the Lichchhavi dynasty had already become extinct with the death of Vasantadeva II who is mentioned as a past king [*āsīt*]. In the reign of Jayadeva II, the Ṭhākurīs alone come to possess the whole kingdom solely. We do not find any trace in inscriptions or in the Vaṁśāvalīs of any successor of Vasantadeva II in the Lichchhavi line.

The mysterious reason for omitting 11 Lichchhavi kings between Jayadeva I and Vṛishadeva is the well-established Hindu historical custom (as in the Purāṇas) to omit names of kings in a dynasty when they cease to be independent. The Guptas exercised dominion over Nepal from Samudra Gupta downwards. Hence we find only Jayadeva I mentioned, who according to the chronology set out above and calculated also by Fleet, flourished in the time of Samudra Gupta. For the time of Samudra Gupta we have his Allahabad inscription proving that Nepal was one of the tributary states in the class which were in close touch with the Imperial Government, paying regular tribute (*kara*). There is nothing to indicate that there happened any change in that condition under Chandra Gupta II and his immediate imperial successors. Either in the reign of Kumāra Gupta I or Skanda-Gupta, we find Haradatta establishing Vaishṇavism in Nepal and actually copying Gupta architecture. His pillar of Garuḍa has the exact formula of Gupta pillars[1] and the Garuḍa is a copy of the Guptan Garuḍa[2]—a human figure with wigs, —which implies that Haradattadeva was owning the imperial Gupta suzerainty. When the Gupta Empire breaks up on account of the rise of the empire of the Maukharis (*c.* 550 A.D.—570 A.D.) we find Mānadeva I (576 A.D.) striking his own coin in Nepal. But this attempt was short-lived, for we

[1] See description in IA, IX. 163. "Its lower half is square, half of the upper part is octagonal, higher up it becomes sixteen-cornered, and finally round." It is about 20 ft. high.

An inscription was inscribed on it later by Mānadeva III, while the pillar stood. It has no reference to the pillar itself. The shrine existed before Aṁśuvarman who made a provision for it in his Harigaon writ of year 32 (Lévi, iii. 94, line 7; the original name was *Dolaśikharasvāmin*, the hill being called *dola*, 'swing').

I found fragments of Gupta sculptures there and have brought one piece to the Patna Museum.

For Gupta writing of the fourth and fifth centuries in Nepal, see Bendall's *Journey*, p. 5.

[2] That is the Garudamadanka.

find the Nepal Guptas asserting sovereignty in the last quarter of the 6th century—an assertion which lasted down to the time of Śivadeva I and Aṁśuvarman.

Out of this list these names mark changes in the religious history of Nepal :

Haridatta (deva)—about 450 A.D., like the Imperial Guptas in the plains made Vaishṇavism the royal cult of Nepal.

Mānadeva I to Vṛishadeva—Buddhism reigned supreme after the Imperial Gupta influence, disappeared in the reign of Mānadeva I (576 A.D.). Coming after the Śaiva Aṁśuvarman who patronised Buddhism merely as a ruler, Vṛishadeva about 660 A.D. made Buddhism again popular (*Sugataśāsana-pakshapātī*, I.A., IX. 178). But his son Śaṅkaradeva, about 680 A.D., is regarded as a second Śaṅkarāchārya for having revived Śaivism at the cost of Buddhism. He has left his monuments at Paśupati and is universally credited by the Buddhists to have abolished monasticism in Nepal Buddhism (Mahāyāna), forcing every *Bhikshu* to lead married life. There have been no wifeless Bhikshus in Nepal ever since; the vihāras are occupied by married Buddhist priests.

After Śaṅkaradeva the Lichchhavis remain markedly Śaiva and Vaishṇavite.

The greatest figure in the period is Dharmadeva. His son Mānadeva III, who in the very year of his accession (705 A.D.) marched against the Mallas, to meet whom since the time of Śivadeva I (yr. 320, Lévi, iii, 69, 107) there had been a

Malla-kara impost in Nepal, records that his father had set up four Pillars of Victory. The reason for this we get from Tibetan History as recorded by the Chinese (translated in JRAS, 1880; 438, 456). The king of Nepal snapped the Tibetan suzerainty brought over Nepal by Narendradeva (643-657 A.D.). He gave battle to the Tibetan king (Ch'inush silung) and killed him (705 A.D.).

We find Śivadeva II employing imperial title in his inscription of 714 A.D., which means that Mānadeva III in his later years was reduced to the position of a *rājan* (as in his inscriptions), the real power passing to the Ṭhākurī line. It was during the minority of Śivadeva II that Vṛishadeva, Śaṅkaradeva and Dharmadeva revived the Lichchhavi line and its prestige.

VI—Data of the Manjusri History on Nepal

On the history of Nepal we have a valuable source in the *Mañjuśrī-mūla-kalpa* in its book on Indian History. The text, edited with the help of the Tibetan translation [my *Mañjuśrī Imperial History*, § 12, p. 40] is as follows :

भविष्यति तदा काले उत्तरां दिशिमाश्भुतः ।
नेपालमण्डले ख्याते हिमाद्रेः कुक्षिमाश्रिते ॥५४९॥
राजा मानवेन्द्रस्तु लिच्छवीनां कुलोद्भवः ।
सोऽपि मन्त्रार्थ-सिद्धस्तु महाभोगी भविष्यति ॥५५०॥
विद्या भोगवती नाम तस्य सिद्धा नराधिपे ।
अशीतिवर्षाणि कृत्वासौ राज्यं तस्करवर्जितम् ॥५५१॥
ततः प्राणात्यये नृपतौ स्वर्गलोके जजग्मसु ।
तत्र मन्त्राशु सिद्धयन्ति शीतला शान्तिकपौष्टिका ॥५५२॥

तारा च लोकविख्याता देवी पण्डरवासिनी।
महाश्वेता परहितोद्युक्ता अखिन्नमनसां सदा ॥५५३॥
इत्येवमादयो प्रोक्ता बहुधा नपतयोस्तदा।
अनेकधा बहुधाश्चैव नानारूपविवर्णिताः ॥५५४॥
शास्तुपूजकास्तेऽपि म्लेच्छराजान् हैं।
T.453 b. ववियः सुवृषश्चैव भावसु शुभसुस्तथा ॥५५५॥
भाक्रमः पदक्रमश्चैव कमलश्चैव कीर्त्यते।
भागुप्तः वत्सकश्चैव (भास्वांश्चैव) पश्चिमः ॥५५६॥

[§ 12 b. Fall of Nepal]

G.६२२ उदयः जिह्नुनो ह्यन्ते म्लेच्छानां विविधास्तथा।
अम्भोधेः भ्रष्टमर्य्यादा बहिःप्राज्ञोपभोजिनः ॥५५७॥
शस्त्रसम्पातविध्वस्ता नेपालाधिपतिस्तदा।
विद्यालुप्ता लुप्तराजानो म्लेच्छतस्करसेविनः ॥५५८॥

५४९, देववन् (ल्ह-ल्दन्)। ५५०. मानवदेवस्तु। ५५४. नृपतयस्तदा। ५५५. हिमवद्वासिनः। वृषः। भूभासः सुभूभासस्तथा। ५५६. पराक्रमः (फ-रोल्-ग्नोद्-ञिद्)। भूगुप्तः (स-स्रुङ=भूपालः)। ५५७. ङङ-छुल् (शीली, जिष्णुः)। ततः परं (दे-ऽोग्)। परपुरुषोपसेविनः (फ्यि-रोल्-सृक्ये द्गुप्स्त्-ञो-वर्-स्प्योद्)। ५५८. विलुप्तास्तत्र राजानो। ५५९. देव-द्विज-प्रियाः।

[§ 12 c. Revival of Nepal]

अनेका भूपतयो प्रोक्ता नाना चैव द्विजप्रिया।
भविष्यन्ति तदा काले चीनं प्राप्य समन्ततः ॥५५९॥

The Mañjuśrī History (§ 12, text, p. 40) says :

(1) At that time in the North, in Nepāla-maṇḍala, in the valley of the Himālaya, there will be king *Māna-vendra* (read *Māna-deva*) born of the dynasty of the Lichchhavis. He would be very prosperous (*mahābhogī*)—the Vidyā Bhogavatī will be established in that king. For eighty years he ruled and made the country free from robbers (549-551) (*Here follow the names of certain goddesses* (552-53).

(2) Then there will be various (*bahudhā*) kings (*dynasties*) several and various (*anekadhā* and *bahudhā*), of various castes (? *nānā-rūpa-vivarṇitāḥ*)—they will be all Buddhists, and foreigners (*mlechcha-rājānaḥ*; Tibetan : Himālayan races or residents).

(3) *Vṛisha*; *Suvṛisha*; *Bhāvasu* (T.—*Bhūbhāsa*); *Śubhasu* (T.—*Subhūbhāsa*); *Bhākrama* (T.—*Parākrama*); *Kamala*; *Bhāgupta* (T.—*Bhūgupta*); *Vatsaka*; [*Aṁśuvarman*, T.—*Bhāsvān*] the Western (535-56).

(4) *Udaya* and *Jishṇu* in the end. After that (Tibetan-*tataḥ paraṁ*) there arose several kings under the Mlechchhas who broke all rules (*bhraṣhṭa-maryādā*) and were dependants of outsiders (T.) (557).

(5) Then the overlord of Nepal (*Nepalādhipatiḥ*) was defeated and killed in battle (by arms); the kings who had lost Vidyās, servants of the Mlechchha robbers, disappeared. There will be several kings, lovers of (Hindu) Gods and Brahmins, having)China (Tibet) on their frontier (558-559).

The above data are highly important, as they give a tale different from the Vaṁśāvalīs, and in accord with Chinese history and inscriptions. Section (1) gives the successful rule of Mānadeva I. His goddess *Bhogavatī* is undoubtedly the *Srī-Bhoginī* on the *Mānāṅka* coin. Section (2) mentions various contemporary dynasties which rose to power in Nepal after Mānadeva I. One of them is headed and represented by *Vṛisha* in whom we may recognize the Lichchhavi Vṛishadeva. *Bhāvasu Subhasu, Bhākrama* and *Kamala* seems to represent some Kirāta family, while *Bhūgupta* corresponds to the Vaṁśāvalī *Bhūmigupta*, the last of the 'Aheer Guptas', who was defeated by Sivadeva I or Aṁśuvarman whom Sivadeva I credits with victories on his enemies. Vatsaka is unrecorded otherwise, but seems to be connected with Bhūgupta. Another contemporary is Aṁśuvarman (of the West) whose name is lost in the Sanskrit text but is supplied from the Tibetan translation. We find Aṁśuvarman in his inscriptions ruling over the Government (*adhikaraṇa*) of the West. It seems that apart from the Guptas there arose at least one more local family to power, and the kingdom after Mānadeva I was sorely torn to pieces, and that it was reunited by Aṁśuvarman under Śivadeva. Aṁśuvarman set up the government of the West with full powers of sovereignty. Vṛishadeva and Aṁśuvarman are treated as contemporaries.

(4) Udaya and Jishṇu (Gupta) are placed at the end of this list and noted to have been the last independent sovereigns of Nepal. After Jishṇu the country passed under the domination of the Mlechchhas, i.e. the Tibetans, until the overlord of Nepal, that is, the Tibetan king, was killed in battle. Then followed Brahmanical kings—a description fully true of the kings from Dharma deva to Vasanta [sena], Śivadeva II and Jayadeva II. The defeat and killing of the Tibetan overlord (705 A. D.) is borne out by Chinese History (JRAS, 1880, 438; V. Smith, EH., 381).

Who was **Vatsaka?**

We have seen that the two Gupta lists in the Vaṁśāvalīs really constitute one series.[1] The first

[1] See section VII of this study.

list is from Jaya Gupta I to Jaya Gupta II—8 rulers (Lévi, II, 72; IA, VII. 89). Jaya Gupta II settled down, according to Kirkpatrick's Vaṁśāvalī, near Janakpur (Tarai). His name is omitted in the Nepal list by other Vaṁśāvalīs, where Yaksha Gupta is the last Nepal Gupta. We find base gold and copper coins of Jaya Gupta II (in characters of circa 600 A. D.), and a mould to forge his gold coins has been discovered in Nālandā excavations this year. This verifies the truth of the Vaṁśāvalī datum about the Gupta dynasty of Nepal. The Vaṁśāvalīs have the following kings in the two lists:—

(Bhagwanlal, Wright, Lévi) [within the Lichchhavi list]	(Kirkpatrick)	
Bhīmadeva	*Bhīmadeva*	(displaced by Aheers, IA, VII. 90)
Vishṇudeva	*Vishṇu Gupta*	

which corresponds with the Gupta list

5. *Bhīma Gupta*
6. *Mati* (or, *Maṇi*) *Gupta*
7. *Vishṇu Gupta*

It seems that up to Bhīma Gupta there was one line of the Guptas who were displaced by the other line beginning with Vishṇu Gupta. Mati-Gupta or Maṇi Gupta was a prince of the displaced line.

Kirkpatrick's Vaṁśāvalī gives two more names after Vishṇu Gupta

Kisnu Gupta
Bhūmi Gupta

These names are not found in the other Vaṁśāvalīs, probably *Kishnu Gupta* is a misreading and duplication of *Vishṇu Gupta*, but *Bhūmi Gupta* is supported by the Mañjuśrī History which has

Bhū Gupta
Vatsaka

In the other list the Vaṁśavalīs after Vishṇu Gupta have

Yaksha Gupta

It seems that after Vishṇu Gupta there were probably two branches:

Vishṇu Gupta
|
Yaksha Gupta — Bhūmi Gupta

That is, *Yaksha Gupta* of the Vaṁśāvalīs would correspond with the *Vatsaka* of the Mañjuśrīmūla kalpa. *Vatsaka* seems to be a nickname.

Now we are helped here by Nepal coins on the identification of *Yaksha Gupta*. We know from the description of Nepal coinage in the Chinese History that in 643 A. D. the Chinese noticed the coin which agrees exclusively with the coin of *Vaiśravaṇa*—'*man on one side, and bull on the other.*'[1] This coin therefore must belong to a king who flourished before 643 A. D. He thus would be either a contemporary or a predecessor of Aṁśuvarman. There is no doubt that Aṁśuvarman imitates this coin by adopting *Kāmadohī*[2] (Kāmadhenu) with the calf at udders on his

[1] See below sec. VIII. The reading on the Vaiśravaṇa coin is *Vaiśravaṇaḥ*—see plate I. 4 of Mr. Walsh, JRAS, 1908, 669.

[2] Not *Kāmadehī*, as formerly read. The corrected reading is by the Rājaguru Pt. Hemarāja Śarmā. *Kāmadohī* = Skt. *Kāma-*

coin. The coin must therefore belong either to Śivadeva I or some other contemporary. The legend on the coin *Vaiśravaṇaḥ* suggests that it was struck by Yaksha Gupta. '*Vaiśravaṇa*' may very well stand as rebus, as Vaiśravaṇa is the king of the Yakshas. His nickname *Vatsaka* ('little calf') probably originated from his representation on the coin as the little calf attached to the Kāmadhenu. It is also possible that he had a second official name as *Vaiśravaṇa*.

The Gupta list would stand thus—

NEPAL

5	Bhīma Gupta	*c.* 575 A. D.
7	Vishṇu Gupta	*c.* 600 A. D.
8	Bhūmi Gupta	*c.* 625 A. D.
8*a*	Yaksha Gupta	*c.* 625 A. D.
[Tarāi]		
8*b*	Jaya Gupta II	*c.* 625 or 640 A. D.

VII—THE GUPTA DYNASTIES OF NEPAL

There are two Gupta Dynasties noted in Nepal histories, and both are confirmed by coins and other evidence. The coins establish their connexion with the Imperial Guptas.

All the Vaṁśāvalīs state that the history of Nepal begins with the '*Gupta Dynasty*' who were of the Goālā caste [Sanskritised in some as *gopāla*][1].

dhuk. It represents the country [of Nepal]—cf. the political maxim :

राजन् दुधुक्षसि यदि क्षितिधेनुमेनां तेनाद्य वत्समिव लोकममुं पुषाण ।

[1] Wright's *History of Nepāl*, 107-109; Bhagwanlal Indraji, XIII, *IA*, 411-12; Lévi, *Nepal*, ii. 72, 74; *Cf.* Kirkpatrick,

This dynasty which is specifically given the name of the Gupta Dynasty, consists of eight names and its first name is lost which is replaced by a phrase *bhuktamānagata* meaning '*the elapsed years of the reign*.' After this dynasty the Vaṁśāvalīs introduce a dynasty of three names and call them the Aheers (Ahīrs) 'from the plains of Hindustan.' The oldest authority, namely the one cited by Kirkpatrick in 1793 A. D., definitely says that they were Rajpūt descendants from *Mahīpa Gopāla* (King Cowherd), that they levied their army in the country situated between Simraongarh and Janakpur (Tarai) and entered and subjugated Nepal. This authority therefore states that the so-called Ahīrs were only a branch of the dynasty which Kirkpatrick has left unnamed and which is officially designated as the *Gupta Dynasty* in the Vaṁśavalīs. There is thus no distinction historically between the Goālās and Ahīrs, as there is none between the two terms—*Goālā* and *Ahīr*. The descendants of these so-called Ahīrs are once more given in the Lichchhavi list above Ś i v a d e v a I and A ṁ ś u v a r m a n, by whom they were finally driven out of Nepal. There are therefore practically two lists of these Guptas (the Goālā-Ahīrs). Their chronology may be calculated back from the known date of Aṁsuvarman and Śivadeva I. When the Nepal histories say that the Gupta-Ahīr line was broken by the Kirātas it should be taken to refer to a Kirāta revival three generations above Aṁśuvarman. The introduction into the Gupta-Ahīr-Aṁśuvarman

Historical Sketch of Nepal in his *Account of the Kingdom of Nepal* (1811), 255-257.

chronology, of the long line of the Kirātas who flourished before and after Aśoka is a result of confusion. The two Kirāta lines—(1) the pre-Christ Kirātas and (2) the pre-Aṁśuvarman Kirātas—have been mixed up together. Nepal History should have and would have begun with the Kirāta Dynasty and not with the Guptas but for that confusion. The Kirātas who intervene just before the line of Aṁśuvarman are called "Yellung Kirāta" in Kirkpatrick and *Ya-laṁva* in Lévi's edition[1] which is treated as the proper name of the first king. *Ya-laṁva* is most likely the ethnic name *Limbu*, a well-known division of the Kirātas still on the eastern frontiers of Nepal. The next name *Pavi* of the Vaniśāvalî is noted in the Mañjuśrī History (p. 40, text)[2] as *Vavi-sha*, placed between M ā n a d e v a I and V ṛ i s h a (d e v a), as a Himālayan Mlechchha and Buddhist by religion.

The Gupta lists and their chronology should be arranged as follows:

(*A*)

1. Jaya Gupta I
2. Parama Gupta
3. Harsha Gupta
4. Bhīma Gupta
5. Mati [or Maṇi] Gupta
6. Vishṇu Gupta
7. Yaksha Gupta

   Jaya Gupta II [K.]

[1] Lèvi, ii. 78, corresponding to *Ya-Lambasa* of Wright.
[2] See extract in § VI above.

(*B*) *Branch of the above*

1. Vara-siṁha
2. Jaya-Mati siṁha [Jaya-Siṁha K.]
3. Bhowany (K.) or
   Bhuvana-siṁha.

(*C*) *Their descendants, mentioned in the Lichchhavi list*[1]

1. Bhīma (deva)
2. [Vishṇu Gupta (K.); *Vishṇu deva*-others]
   [Kishnoo Gupta (only in K.)]
3. Viśva Gupta (L.) (*Viśva deva*-others; father-in-law of Aṁśuvarman)
4. Bhūmi Gupta (only in K.) but confirmed by Mañjuśrī History, whih gives Bhū Gupta as a contemporary of Aṁsuvarman

It seems that from *Bhīma Gupta* (A, no. 4; C, 1) lines branched off. No. 6 of A corresponds with no. 2 of C; and no. 5 of A corresponds with no. 2 of B.

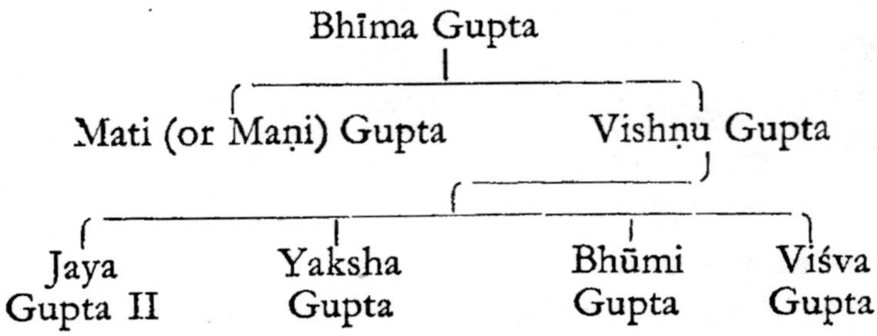

The dates assignable to the Gupta dynasty of Nepal, composed of section A and C, would be :

[1] Bhagwanlal Indraji, XIII, *IA*, 412, ii. Lévi 74, Wright, 109, Kirkpatrick, 256.

[1] 13 IA 413; 2 Lévi 122; Wright, 130; Kirkpatrick, 260-61.

Jayagupta I	*c.* 500 A.D.	
Parama Gupta	*c.* 525 A.D.	
Harsha Gupta,	*c.* 550 A.D.	
Bhīma Gupta	*c.* 575 A.D.	dispossessed by the Lichchhavis [probably by Mānadeva I who succeeded in 576 A.D.]
Vishṇu Gupta	*c.* 600 A.D.	He actually reigned in the valley; his endowment *Vishṇu-nātha* still exists 8 miles north of Kathmandu[1]
Jaya Gupta II Yaksha Gupta Viśva Gupta Bhūmi Gupta		
	c. 625 A.D.	the time of the conquest of Aṁśuvarman under Śivadeva I who is noted to have expelled them

As to the position of Section B, it is certain that they had their seat in the Tarai. There being no room for them from 500 A.D. to 600 A.D.—they, —another branch of the same family—the *Mahīpāla gopāla* i.e. the 'Imperial Guptas'—must come after Jaya Gupta II, when the family was dispossessed in Nepal, in other words, after 625 A.D.

VIII—Coinage

Coins of Nepal Guptas

This is confirmed by the gold coins of Varasiṁha which have been assigned to the seventh century, Allan opining that they '*cannot be before the*

[1] Kirkpatrick, 191.

seventh century; nothing is known of their attribution.' The coins are illustrated in V. Smith's Catalogue of the Indian Museum, pl. xvi. 14. and Allan's Gupta Coins (British Museum) pl. xxiv. 11. The legend is read doubtfully by Rapson as "*Vīra* [-*sena* or *siṁha*]".[1] It has "*Kramādityaḥ*" on the reverse. On the obverse there is a cow in the style of the Kāmadhenu of the Nepal coins of Vaiśravaṇa and Aṁśuvarman. Dr. V. Smith could not decide between "bull? or cow,"[2] an uncertainty which will be caused to everyone who would be introduced first to the Nepal Kāmadohī. The name is *Śrī Vara* [*siṁha*]. Although certainly related to the Imperial Gupta coinage, the coin of Varasiṁha, has the weight not of the Gupta system but of Nepal coins, the weight of the three gold coins of Varasiṁha being 162.3, 162.5, and 169 grs. which as Smith says is 'abnormal' and 'not easy to explain' (p. 98). It is explainable only on the weight system of Nepal which we find there in vogue in the coinage of Vaiśravaṇa and Aṁśuvarman (Cunningham, CAI., xiii, 3, wt. 172; xiii, 6, wt. 169 grs.).

Varasiṁha in dispossessing Jaya Gupta II must be taken to have dispossessed him in the Tarai. Only three coins of Varasiṁha have been found up to this time, and one of them was obtained by Col. Rivett-Carnak at Benares. His coins should be looked for in Champaran. We know now about Jaya Gupta II's coins that they were current

[1] JRAS, 1900, 131.
[2] p. 122.

near Magadha, as a mould to forge his gold coin has been just discovered (dug out) at Nālandā.[1] His principality must have been near Nālandā wherefrom the coin could be passed into the territory of its circulation or it could be discounted even in Magadha as that of a recognized feudatory. Jaya Gupta's coins are the most debased gold coins of the whole of the Gupta series, having only $\frac{1}{5}$ gold, which shows that he was in terrible financial straits. We have both his copper and gold coins. His title on his coins is *Prakāṇḍayaśaḥ*. His copper coins have the Imperial Garuḍa, proving that he belonged to the Imperial Gupta family. His coins have been assigned by V. Smith to *c.* 600 A.D.[2]

VIII.—Lichchhavi Coinage

It seems that on the weakness of the Gupta imperial organization [*c.* 500 A.D.] a branch from Magadha or North Bihar entered into Nepal and took direct possession of Nepal. The Lichchhavis then naturally became direct subordinates to the local Guptas. About 576 A.D. Mānadeva I reasserted the independence of the Lichchhavi dynasty and struck his coins. He was followed by Guṇadeva (or Guṇa-kāma-deva) of the Guṇāṅka coins. They are a twin system of [*Mānāṅka-Guṇāṅka*] coinage. The names Mānadeva and Guṇa-

[1] This was brought to me by Mr. G. C. Chandra, Supdt. A.S.,C.C. to be deciphered. This is exactly of the type illustrated by Cunningham in CMI, pl. II. 3. The mould is made from a coin.

[2] V. Smith, CIM, p. 121; Cunningham, CMI, pl. II, 3; Allan, 153.

k ā m a - d e v a were transferred from between V a s a n t a d e v a I and S i v a d e v a I to a position below V a s a n t a d e v a II and above S i v a d e v a II in the Lichchhavi list. The confusion was caused by the appearance of M ā n a - d e v a II (contemporary and sovereign of J i s h ṇ u - G u p t a) there between V a s a n t a d e v a - U d a - y a d e v a and S i v a d e v a II. This led to the transposition of Mānadeva I and Guṇakāmadeva as nos. 25 and 26 of the Lichchhavi list from their original position between nos. 15 (Vasantadeva I) and 16 (Sivadeva I).[1]

On the evidence of coins there seems to be an assertion by the Lichchhavis in the time of M ā n a - d e v a I who coins his money. Now the Mañjuśrī Imperial History supplies the numismatic identification of the female figure on the coins of this king: *Srī-Bhoginī.* It says that the Vidyā worshipped by Mānadeva (who lived before Vṛishadeva) was *Bhogavatī.* Mañjuśrī's Imperial History begins the Lichchhavi line with him, for he was the first to become independent of the Imperial Guptas. The coin of G u ṇ a follows immediately M ā n a d e v a ' s coin. But we gather from the coin of V a i ś r a va ṇ a that the family had again a set-back. There is no room for this last coin after A ṁ ś u v a r m a n and the coin of Aṁśuvarman and that of Vaiśravaṇa are so connected that one must follow the other. The design of *Kāmadohī* (the reading as corrected from *Kāmadehī* by the Rājaguru Pandit H e m a -

[1] 13 IA, 412.

rāja Sarmā) appears on these two coins only. Aṁśuvarman's successor Jishṇu Gupta abandons it, and the *Paśupati* series which follows Jishṇu Gupta[1] abandons it. If it came after the Paśupati series—its date would be *c.* 800 A.D. which will be too late for the script of the Vaiśravaṇa coin. The coin should therefore come before Aṁśuvarman and after Mānāṅka and Guṇāṅka coins, where it has been already placed by numismatists (see Cunningham, C. A. I. 116). But as there is no name in the Lichchhavi list to whom it can be assigned, it has remained unassigned. We may take it to belong to 'the revived (Ahīr) Gupta dynasty,' where it can belong either to Yaksha Gupta or Bhūmi Gupta. '*Yaksha*' corresponds to '*Vaiśravaṇa*,' the king of the Yakshas. The legend acts as the rebus, if not the actual regnal name of the king. It may be safely presumed that the line of Vṛishadeva, Śaṅkaradeva, Dharmadeva, etc.—strikes the Paśupati coins under the new Śaiva influence, in the name of their Deity, *Paśupati*, with changing symbols—the Trident probably signifying the reign of Sankaradeva who dedicated the large trident noted in Nepal history and come down to our time. His son is accredited to have donated the copper *Nandi* at Paśupati. The Sun symbol on the Paśupati series denotes the Sūryavaṁśa of the Lichchhavis. The Paśupati coinage has 'six distinct types'[1] and from Vṛishadeva to Vasantadeva we have 6 kings.

[1] E. H. Walsh, J.R.A.S., 1908, 681.

In weight the Vaiśravaṇa coin does not belong to the series of Paśupati, but to that of Mānāṅka, Guṇānka and Aṁśuvarman. The Paśupati series is subsequent to Vaiśravana.[1]

Chinese History on Nepal Coinage

The Chinese have described the coinage of Nepal about 643-651 A. D. Wang-Hiuen-t'se, in his description[2] of the kingdom of Nepal under king Narendradeva, relates that Nepal "*has copper money which bears on one side the figure of a man and on the reverse a horse.*" In the other edition of the Thang history (called *The New History*), the description of the money is "*on one side it bears the figure of a man and the reverse a horse and a bull, and has no hole in the middle*" (that is, unlike Chinese coins).

This description is only applicable to the following coins:

(1) Coin of *Vaiśravaṇa* (Cunningham, C.A.I., pl. XIII, 3; Walsh, JRAS, 1908, p. 669, pl. I. 4). Here there is on the obverse what Cunningham describes—"*The types* [of Nepal coins] *are few in number. The principal type shows the king seated on a throne holding a flower in his right hand*" (p. 114) also further—"*Deity or Raja, seated to front*" (p. 116). The reverse has a cow (not bull). The very small calf is mostly very indistinct—e.g. on the coin illustrated by Mr. Walsh where letters and other features of the coin are all clear but the calf is difficult to distinguish. The cow

[1] E. H. Walsh, J.R.A.S., 1908, 681.

[2] Preserved in the History of the Thang Dynasty ; *J. A.*, 1894, 66. The passage has been translated several times. See Lévi's citation, *Nepal*, i. 163-64; n2 at p. 164.

is so drawn that by a man in the street it may be taken as a bull.

(2) Coin of M ā n a d e v a I (*Mānāṅka*) where the figure of the goddess *Bhoginī* may well be mistaken for that of a man (see Mr. Walsh's plate, fig. 1). The griffin on the reverse has the perfect appearance of a horse.

(3) Aṁśuvarman's series having on one side the cow [which can be mistaken for a bull] and on the other the 'horse' (really griffin) (CAI, xiii. 4; Walsh, I. 5) is the only other nearest approach, but probably it has to be ruled out for not having any human figure. Jishṇu Gupta's coin has similarly to go out, because it has the griffin on one side but no human figure or the cow on the other side but *vajra* in a decorative style.

Hence the Chinese party who saw Nepalese copper coins in 643 to 651 A.D. based their description on the coins of M ā n a d e v a I, V a i ś r a v a ṇ a, and also possibly of A ṁ ś u v a r m a n ('New History' : '*horse and bull*'). It seems that *Mānāṅka*, *Vaiśravaṇa* and Aṁśuvarman's coins had been largely minted and they mainly supplied the needs of currency up to *c.* 650 A. D.

The value of copper in the Madhyadeśa (*Madhes* of the present-day Nepalese) was $\frac{1}{18}$th of silver, but probably in Nepal it was still more dear. J i s h ṇ u - G u p t a ' s inscription at Thankot[1] calculates all

[1] Lévi, *Nepal*, iii. 104 (lines 23-25, p. 107 : kare cha yena kārshāpaṇan deyan tenāshṭau paṇā deyā yenāushṭau paṇā deyaṃ tena paṇa-chatushṭayaṃ Malla-kare cha paṇa-chatushṭa-yan deyaṃ.

taxes in Kārshāpaṇas, which confirms the Chinese testimony of a copper currency. So does also the fact that we have found no silver coin of the period in Nepal. But Aṁśuvarman's inscription of the year 30,[1] mentions both *pu.* (i.e. *purāṇa* = silver punch-marked pieces) and *pa.* i.e., *paṇa.* It is possible that the reference is only for the purposes of calculation into Kārshāpaṇas. In any case silver was rare in Nepal.[2]

On the vexed question of the date of Nepal coins, the Chinese description is evidence of that the age of the Mānāṅka and Vaiśravaṇa coins cannot be later than 643 A. D. and that Paśupati coins had not come on the scene yet and that they have to be dated after 651 A. D.

It is not possible for the Mānāṅka coin to belong to Mānadeva II, contemporary of Jishṇu Gupta, as he ruled for a year or so, and could not leave so numerous a series, nor of course can it belong to Mānadeva III [of the Changu Narayan inscription] who came half a century later.

[On the absence of Nepal coinage between *c.* 800 to 1300 A. D., the discussion is to be found in this thesis in § XII].

[1] Lévi, *ibid*, p. 93 (Harigaon insc.).

[2] The T'ang History mentions silver in Tibet in the same period. See Bushell's translation, JRAS, 1880, p. 442—"*They have abundance of gold, silver, copper and tin.*"

IX—Dynastic Revolution on the death of Amsuvarman

The Line of Udayadeva

The line of Udayadeva is a puzzle. It is given both in the inscription of Jayadeva II, great grandson of Udayadeva, as if it belongs to the Lichchhavis. It is given in the Vaṁśavalīs as the concluding portion of the Lichchhavis line. The puzzle is solved by Chinese datum to be discussed below and the Thankot inscription of Jishṇu Gupta mentioning a Mānadeva, not as 'the banner of the Lichchhavi dynasty' the usual dynastic description, but as 'the banner of the dynasty seated on the throne' (*singhāsanādhyāsi-kula-ketu*).[1] It is necessary to remember throughout these discussions that according to one view—e.g. Lévi's—Aṁśuvarman married the daughter of Śivadeva (the name *Viśva* supposed to be a corruption of *Śiva*), and according to the other as noted in a Vaṁśāvalī in possession of the Baḍā Kāzi of Nepal (cited in Landon, ii, 315) Aṁśuvarman was adopted by Śivadeva as a son, who was some sort of a nephew to him. The inscriptions do not however show that Śivadeva treated Aṁśuvarman as his son, but this by itself is not sufficient. The name ending-*deva* in the name of *Udaya-deva*, who was in every event the immediate successor of Aṁśuvarman need not trouble us, as Aṁśuvarman's admitted descendants did adopt the *deva*-ending.

[1] Lévi, iii. 107.

What happened on the death of Aṁśuvarman we gather from an unexpected quarter—Chinese history of the T'ang Dynasty. According to the inscription of Jayadeva II, King Udayadeva's son was Narendradeva.[1] About this Narendradeva there is a volume of information in the Chinese history. His dress, his palace [Kailāsakūṭa], the coinage current in his time, and his international status are all described in detail. That account says that the father of the king *Na-ling-ti-po* (*Narendradeva*), whom the Imperial Ambassador met in Nepal in 643 A.D., had been deposed by his (Narendradeva's) uncle, the younger brother of his father; whereupon Narendradeva sought the help of the Tibetan king (Strong-tsan-Gampo) who restored him to the throne of Nepal and made him his vassal. In 651 A.D. Śrī Narendra (*Chi-li-Na-lien-to-lo*) sent a mission to the Chinese Emperor. This was a year later than the death of Strong-tsan-Gampo. Narendradeva was still ruling in 657 A.D. when a Chinese ambassador passed through Nepal[2].

We thus get the definite news that Udayadeva, father of Narendradeva was deposed by his younger brother who became king. Naturally the name of this collateral and usurper is not to be

[1] The reading and interpretation of Bhagwanlal Indraji (I.A., IX, 178) has been corrected by Fleet (G. I., I., 187) which correction I have verified in Nepal. The learned Rāja-Gurn Pt. Hemarāja Śarmā who has gone deep into the matter is of the opinion that it is not possible to maintain the reading *trayodaśa* of Dr. Bhagwanlal Indraji.

[2] J.A., 1894, 63ff; 1900, 302.

found in the genealogy given by the grandson of Narendradeva, Jayadeva II. But we know his name from the inscriptions of Jishṇu Gupta who, three or four years after the last inscription of Aṁśuvarman (dated 40 + 4 or 5), was ruling from the *Kailāsakūṭa* Palace of Aṁśuvarman as the Viceroy of Dhruvadeva who was residing at Mānagṛiha, the palace of the Lichchhavi kings. Before that time Jishṇu Gupta ruled also as the viceroy of Mānadeva (who should be called Mānadeva II as opposed to the later Mānadeva, great-grandson of Vṛishadeva, who should be called Mānadeva III). The date in the inscription at Thankot wherein Mānadeva II is king, is not distinct now[1] but it is not difficult to decide whether Dhruvadeva was the uncle of Narendradeva, or Mānadeva II who dispossessed his father. For Dhruvadeva's date being the year 48 (= 643 A.D.) he must be the latter of the two, as Narendradeva had succeeded by 643 when he was on the throne. Then Dhruvadeva is specifically described as a Lichchhavi, while Mānadeva II is significantly described by a new appellation—'*the banner of the enthroned family*'—i.e., the family of Aṁśuvarman as opposed to that of the Lichchhavis. That also proves that Aṁśuvarman had also assumed full sovereignty in his last year. This is also certain that in the short period between the year 44 of Aṁśuvarman

[1] Lévi reads it doubtfully as 500? But I do not find this figure. On the other hand the date reads like 44, see plate XVII, last line (Lévi, iii)—See my enlarged reproduction herein.

and about 48, and before 643 A.D., Udayadeva was dethroned by Mānadeva II. The Vaṁśāvalīs correctly place *Mānadeva* between Udayadeva and Narendradeva (with the addition of one more name, *Guṇakāma-deva*, after *Mānadeva*, as a mistaken transposition from his place below *Mānadeva* I, for there is no room for Guṇakāmadeva here). Taking four years (the difference between Aṁśuvarman's date 44 and of Jishṇu Gupta 48), Udayadeva at the earliest must have succeeded Aṁśuvarman four years before Narendradeva, 643, i.e. *circa* 639 A.D., and latest in 642-643 A.D.

Now the line of Udayadeva when dated from Chinese data and inscriptions exhibits the ups and downs in the political position of the Lichchhavi-Ṭhākurī line and the pure Lichchhavi line in the following manner:

Lichchhavis

Vṛishadeva
|
Śaṅkaradeva
|
Dharmadeva

} c. 657-705 A.D.
703 Tibetan king defeated and killed by Nepal king

|
Bhaṭṭāraka Mahārāja Mānadeva III
705-732 A.D.
|
Mahîdeva, 732 A.D.
|
Vasantadeva (sena)
415 G. E.=735 A. D.
Bhaṭṭaraka Mahārāja
(subordinate to Jayadeva II) died before yr. 153 [748 A.D.]

Śivadeva I
635 A.D.
|
Daughter (?)
= Aṁśuvarman, or adopted by Śivadeva I., died *c* 639 A.D.

Udayadeva
(*c* 639-643 A.D. deposed)
|
Narendradeva
643-657 A.D.
|
Śivadeva II (yr. 119) 714 A.D.
(minor or posthumous son at his father's death)
Paramabhaṭṭāraka Mahārājādhirāja
|
Paramabhaṭṭāraka Mahārājādhirāja (name gone, yr. 143) Jayadeva II, yr. 153 (748 A.D.)

Mānadeva II [Dhruvadeva] (643 A.D.)
[Both under Jishṇu Gupta's dictatorship]

M ā n a d e v a II and D h r u v a d e v a both had their residence at Mānagṛiha, hence there was no room for V ṛ i s h a d e v a from *c* 639 to 643. N a r e n d r a d e v a was the king of the whole of Nepal in 643 and he was such a king up to 657 at least. Hence V ṛ i s h a d e v a and his line rose to power after N a r e n d r a d e v a and during the minority of Ś i v a d e v a II, whose record we find 63 years later than his father's. During this interval V ṛ i s h a d e v a, S a ñ k a r a d e v a, D h a r m a d e v a, and M ā n a d e v a III succeeded.

D h a r m a d e v a 's position seems to have been great, he set up four Pillars of Victory according to the Changu Narayan inscription of his son M ā n a - d e v a III. This is confirmed by Chinese sources. The king of Nepal killed the Tibetan king in war in 703 A.D. or 705 A.D.[1]

M ā n a d e v a in the beginning of his reign (386 G. E. = 705) carried war against the Mallas and reached the Gandak (North Bihar).[2] But in 732 his position is that he is merely described by a subordinate of his as *Śrīmānadeva-nṛipati* (I.A., IX. 167) while his contemporary Ś i v a d e v a II (119 = 714 A.D.) is styled with Imperial titles *Paramabhaṭṭāraka Mahārājādhirāja* (I.A., IX. 174). And 24 years later, evidently in the reign of J a y a d e v a II the same imperial title still continued in the line, the family employing the Ṭhākurī era, year 143, (I.A., IX, 176); while V a s a n t a d e v a (sena) in 415[3] G. E.=735 A.D. is only *Mahārāja* and a simple (not *parama*) *Bhaṭṭāraka*.

V a s a n t a d e v a must have been dead when J a y a d e v a II in the year 153=748 A.D. said about him '*āsit Vasantadevaḥ*' (I.A, IX, 178).

The Mañjuśrī History correctly records the situation that after U d a y a came J i s h ṇ u

[1] In 703 A.D. according to E. H. Parker, Journal of Manchester Oriental Society, 1911, pp. 129-52, cited by V. Smith, EH., p. 381; 705 A.D. according to Dr. Bushell, JRAS, 1880, 438.

[2] See Changu Narayan inscription, lines recovered by Lévi (iii, 14).

[3] I.A., IX. 167. The figure is 415, not 435; *cf.* plates 3 and 2 for the figure 10 (I.A., IX), and chart of figures in Bendall's Cambridge *Cat.* and Bühler's chart for 30.

and that Jishṇu was the last independent king of Nepal, that the kings after him became subordinate to the Mlechchhas (Tibetans), and that the overlord of Nepal (Tibetan king) having been killed by arms, there arose several kings, lovers of 'Devas' and 'Brāhmaṇas.' These latter were the Lichchhavis of the line of Vṛishadeva. Although Vṛishadeva was a patron of Buddhism, Śaṅkara, Dharma, Mānadeva III and also probably Vasantadeva, and certainly Śivadeva II and Jayadeva II were distinctly Brāhmanical, devotees of Vishṇu and Śiva, to whom their dedicated monuments still survive.

There is no trace of any Tibetan overlordship after 703 A.D. which is a landmark in their international relation—a point entirely missed by Lévi. Their imperial titles of *Paramabhaṭṭāraka* and *Mahārājādhirāja* from 714 to 738 fully establishes their independent position.

The T'ang History, bks. 256—257, gives the contemporary history of Tibet, which has been translated by Dr. S. W. Bushell, physician to the British Legation at Peking, in the Journal of the Royal Asiatic Society, 1880, p. 435ff. According to it, Strong-tsan-Gampo (Chinese—Ch'it-sung-lungtsan) died in 650 and was succeeded by his grandson, aged 8, whose son Ch'inushsilung was killed in his expedition against Nepal and was succeeded by a minor son aged 7 in 705 A.D. It was not until 755-756 (two successions later) that the Tibetan king once more rose to military greatness by attacking China and taking her capital in 756 A.D. Between 740 and 769 A.D. Tibet was defeated by Muktâpîḍa Lalitâditya of Kashmir.[1] Between 822 and 842 Tibet again goes down and a civil war ensues (842), and in 849 Tibet becomes a broken vassal of China. It becomes thus evident that in Dharmadeva's time (703) Tibet is defeated, and down to the time of Jayadeva II (748 A.D.) Nepal was absolutely her own master, there being weakness in Tibet up to 755.[2] *C.* 800 Nepal was strong enough to defeat the great Jayāpīḍa.

It is noteworthy that the family of Mānadeva II is not named by Jishṇu Gupta at Thankot as the *Lichchhavi-kula-ketu*, but as *singhāsanādhyāsi-kula-ketu* (Lévi, iii, 105). This fully confirms the view that Udayadeva and his brother were not technically Lichchhavis, but Ṭhākurīs. It should be noted however that Yuan Chwang regards the kings before Aṁśuvarman and after him (even including Aṁśuvarman) as Lichchhavis. That is, in the Ṭhākurī family the predominant element was the Lichchhavi affiliation.

The date of Narendradeva (643-657) definitely contributes to the ascertainment of the correct date for Aṁśuvarman. He must have

[1] Mon. Lévi has not noticed the Nepalese victory over Tibet of the year 703 A.D. and has gratuitously held Nepal to have been subject to Tibet from the time of Śivadeva I and Aṁśuvarman down to 880 A.D., while the Chinese historians themselves state the Indians states that used to approach China against Tibet ceased to do so at 760 A.D.—S. Julien, J.A. 1842. 2.

[2] V. Smith, EH., 386-87.

died not later than 643, or *minus* 4 or 3 years of Jishṇu Gupta's rule, *c* 640 or 639 A.D.

It was in the time of Narendradeva that Nepal for the first time became a vassal of Tibet, that is, about 643 A.D. This is definitely stated by the Chinese history. This happened as a result of Narendradeva's seeking help of foreign intervention and not as a result of any military invasion. It was Narendradeva who furnished 7000 cavalry to the Chinese ambassador along with the Tibetan force of 1200, to dislodge Arjuna or Aruṇāśva, and not Aṁśuvarman as erroneously stated by Fleet.[1] Narendradeva's name is specifically noted by the Chinese writers in this connection.

It is likely that the marriage of the alleged daughter of Aṁśuvarman with Strong-tsan-Gampo took place, if in 642 A.D. the agreed date, not in the lifetime of Aṁśuvarman but after him and in the period when the Nepalese king was seeking the help of Tibet. If the lady was a sister of Udayadeva, she was the daughter of Aṁśuvarman. If she was a sister of Narendradeva, she was Udayadeva's daughter. The Tibetan word translated as *prabhāvarman* may stand either for *Aṁśuvarman* or *Udaya* (*deva*) *varman*. In the closing years (about the year 44) Aṁśuvarman was *Mahārājādhirāja*. That title, the chronology, and the Chinese records are all against Aṁśuvarman's having accepted the

[1] GI, *I.*, 190.

suzerainty of Tibet. And so is also the express authority of the Mañjuśrī History which definitely dates the foreign domination of Nepal *after* J i s h ṇ u-G u p t a.

X—Architecture, Epigraphy and Constitution

Chinese account of Nepal, 643-651 *A.D.*

[History of the Thang Dynasty, *c.* 221[1]]

People, Currency, Arts, Sciences and Worship

"The kingdom of Nepal is right to the west of Tibet. The inhabitants have the custom to shave their hair just to the level of the eye-brows. They pierce their ears and suspend therein tubes made of bamboo or horn of cattle. It is a mark of beauty to have ears hanging upto the shoulders. They eat with their hands without using spoons or sticks. All their utensils are made of copper. The merchants there, moving and stationary, are numerous; cultivators, rare. They have coins of copper which bear on one side a figure of man and on the reverse a horse [*New History:* They have coins of copper which bear on one side a figure of man and on the reverse a horse and a bull, and which have no hole in the middle]. They do not pierce the noses of their bulls. They clothe themselves with a single piece of cloth which envelopes the body. They bathe themselves several times a day. Their houses are constructed of wood. The walls of these are sculptured and painted. They are very fond of scenic plays, they take pleasure in blow-

[1] J. A. 1894, 65*ff*.

ing trumpets and beating drums. They understand fairly well calculation of destiny and researches in physical philosophy. They are equally clever in the art of the Calendar-maker. They adore five celestial spirits, and sculpture their images in stone. Each day they wash them with purifying water. They roast a lamb and offer it in sacrifice."

The King

"Their king, *Nalingtipo* (Narendradeva) adorns himself with true pearls, rock crystal, mother-of-pearl, coral, and amber; he has in the ears rings of gold and pendants of jade, and a breloc belt ornamented with the figure of the Buddha. He seats himself on a seat of lions.[1] In the middle of the hall one spreads flowers and perfumes. The nobles and the officers and all the court are seated to the right and to the left on the ground; at his sides are ranged hundreds of soldiers having arms."

Kailāsakūṭa Palace in 643-657 A.D.

"In the middle of the palace there is a tower of seven storeys roofed with copper tiles. Its balustrade, grilles, columns, beams, and every thing therein are set with fine and even precious stones. At each of the four corners of the tower there projects a waterpipe of copper. At the base there are golden dragons which spout forth water. From the summit of the tower water is poured through runnels which finds its way down below, streaming like a fountain from the mouth of the golden Makara."

[1] *Cf.* Thankot inscr.—*siṁhāsanâdhyāsi-kulaketu.*

The Vaṁśāvalīs throughout mention the construction of palaces of nine storeys and seven storeys and of copper-roofing temples. The art of Nepal excited the admiration of the Chinese, themselves highly artistic.

Architecture and Temples of Nepal in 657 A. D.

The following passages from Chinese History (translated from French by Dr. Banerji-Sastri) prove that in the year 657 A.D. when the Ambassador Wang Hiuentse passed through Nepal once more (in the reign of Narendradeva whom he had known since 643 A.D.) his companions saw a petroleum spring in the neighbourhood of Kathmandu, which might be rediscovered with profit.

The architectural style which is now known as the pagoda style was already in vogue in Nepal in the middle of the seventh century. The Chinese saw there then such temples and secular buildings, the like of which they had not seen or known in their own country. The style travelled from Nepal to China, and not *vice versa.* The style was not known in China before, while every house in Nepal in its essentials is composed in that style. It was a Nepalese invention, and such is also the opinion of Mr. Landon (ii. 257-58) who can speak on the subject with authority as he studied the question in China also. Throughout Tibet and Mongolia the style is unknown. This shows that in China it was an importation, at first as a Buddhist religious architecture from Nepal.

The passage bearing on the palace of Narendradeva which was no other than the *Kailāsakūṭa*, of which Aṁśuvarman was greatly proud (inscription of the year 34), is cited above. The Vaṁśāvalīs too note the great Palace and Secretariate built by Aṁśuvarman (Wright, p. 133).

Wang Hiuen-ts'e on Nepal

I.—"The *Si-kouo-hing-tchoan* of Wang Hiuen-ts'e says: In the second year of Hien-king (657) an imperial order sent Wang Hiuen-ts'e and some others into the kingdoms of the West to offer to the Buddha a Kaṣāya. They went to *Ni-po-lo* (Nepāla) towards the South-West. Arrived at *Pouo-lo-tou*, they came to the east of the village at the bottom of a depression. There was there a small lake of water on fire. If one takes in hand some lighted fire to illuminate it, suddenly on its surface appears a luminous fire which emerges from the very bosom of the water. If one wishes to extinguish it by drenching it with the water, the water changes into fire and burns. The Chinese envoy and his followers placed thereon a cooking vessel and thus prepared their nourishment by heating. The envoy interrogated the king of the country; the king replied to him : Yore, in striking strokes with a staff, one made to appear a chest of gold; order was given to a man to drag it out. But each time that one pulled it out, it replunged. Tradition says that it is the gold of the diadem of *Mi-le P'ou-sa* (Maitreya Bodhisattva), who is due to come to complete the path. The Nāga of fire protects it and defends it; the fire of this lake is the fire of the Nāga of Fire."[1]

II.—"To the South-East of the capital, at a small distance, there is a lake of water and of fire. In going one li towards the East, one finds the fountain *A-ki-po-li*[2] (the *Fa-youen-tchou-lin* bears: *A-ki-po-mi*; the same alternations in the two redactions of the *History of the T'angs*). Its circumference is of 20 pou (40 paces). In the dry time as in the season of the rains, it is deep; it does not dissipate but keeps on steaming always. If one holds in hand some lighted fire, the entire tank takes fire; the smokes and the fire rise several feet high. If one drenches this fire with some water, then the fire becomes more intense. If one launches therein powdered dust, the flame ceases and what one throws therein turns to ash. If one places a cooking vessel over the water to prepare the food by heating, it is well-heated. There was in olden time in this fountain a coffer of gold. A king ordered to drag this coffer out. When one had brought it out of the mud, the men and elephants pulled at it without succeeding in making it come out. And in the night a supernatural voice says : Here is the diadem of Maitreya Buddha; creatures could not assuredly obtain it, because the Nāga of Fire guards it."

"To the South of the town, at more than 10 li, is found an isolated mountain covered with an extraordinary vegetation; Temples are disposed there in numerous storeys which one would take for a crown

[1] *Missions of Wang*—Fragment IV, drawn from *Fa-youen-tchou-lin*, chap. xvi, p. 15b, col. 17.

[2] *Agni-purī*, or *agni-pushkarī*—K. P. J.

of clouds. Under the pines and the bamboos, the fishes and the dragons follow man, tame and confiding. They approach the man and come to receive what to eat. Who does them violence causes the ruin of those his own."

"Recently the orders of the Empire passed by this kingdom and thence extended far. Now it depends on *T'eu-fan* (Tibet)."[1]

III.—"In the capital of Nepal there is a construction in storeys which has more than 200 tch'eu of height and 80 peu (400 feet) of circumference. Ten thousand men can find place in its upper part. It is divided in three terraces[2] and each terrace is divided in seven storeys. In the four pavilions, there are sculptures to make you marvel. Stones and pearls decorate them."[3]

Epigraphy of Nepal of the 7th and 8th centuries

Epigraphy of Nepal is a peculiar matter—it is puzzling, especially when one first takes to it. Writing in Nepal is very stationary, the result being that epigraphs of the seventh century appear to be older by several centuries, judged from the standard of the plains. This led Professor Lévi to assign records dated in Gupta Era to Śaka Era and a supposed Lichchhavi Era. The best authority on Nepal paleography is Dr. Bendall who made a very deep study of manuscript paleography of Nepal and with that knowledge he had no hesitation in

[1] Fragments II and III.

[2] "Court-yards" in the Vaṁśāvalīs (Wright, 133).

[3] *Cheu-kia-fang-tchi.* Cf. *Le Nepal*, per S. Lévi, vol. I, pp. 157-9.

assigning correct dates to Nepal lithic inscriptions. He found Gupta characters of the fourth and fifth centuries which were distinct from the Aṁśuvarman group (*Journey*, p. 5). Outside the Kathmandu group of towns no search has been made at sites of the old seats of governments. The Kailāsakūṭa mound is yet to be excavated.

In the meantime I may emphasize the archaic nature of Nepal epigraphy by citing one example. There is a copy of the law Digest *Kalpataru* of Lakshmīdhara, which was written in the time of the author—12th century. I was anxious to see it, but as the owner General Kaisar Shamsher Jang was away from Nepal I could not see it. My friend the Rājaguru told me that the manuscript which is (on palm leaf) in Nāgarī has notes on the margin of leaves in Gupta characters. Similarly the Rañjana script still current in Nepal is only a variety of Gupta letters. It is so common that ordinary engravers made seals for me in this script.

As Gupta writing persisted in Nepal, so did Guptan and post-Guptan style in sculpture in Nepal. At every step I was deceived by sculptures, a few centuries old, giving an impression of the 9th century and 8th century technique.

Origin of Dual Sovereignty in Nepal

Dual Sovereignty is a bad working hypothesis to the modern political theorist. But it is fully attested and authenticated by the history of Nepal—not only of the period reviewed above but also of the subsequent periods—fully borne out by colophons of manuscripts noted by Bendall (Nepal Catalogue, i, Introduction), by inscriptions [e.g., Bendall's *Journey*, p. 15] and notices in the Vaṁśavalīs of "joint rule"—down to our own time. It is in the very soil of Nepal and works well, wonderfully well. Its origin lies in the dual constitution of the Lichchhavis—of the *Rājā* and *Upa-Rājā*—which they carried from Vaiśāli into Nepal. Even in their Monarchical days they could not shake it off. The curious sight of two sovereigns in the new Svayamabhū nāth inscription[1] and in the Early Ṭhākurī history puzzled me until the Lichchhavi constitution of the republican Vaiśāli was recalled. This *Dvairājya* system which was fully known to Ancient Hindus and which the Jaina sūtras ask their monks to avoid, is suitable for a constitutional oasis like Nepal. It, at the same time, put a limit to her power of expansion.

Nepal in the past, as to this day, has been mainly oligarchical and never purely monarchical. Therein lies both her strength and weakness.

XI—Thakuris after Jayadeva II

The list of the Vaṁśāvalīs[2] for the period 880 A.D. to the present dynasty has been confirmed[3] by the researches of Dr. Bendall based purely on dated

[1] JBORS, XXII. 81.

[2] Bendall's Vaṁśāvalī, *Nepal Cat.* i, p. 21; Bhagwanlal Indraji's ed., I.A., IX. 413, other Vaṁśāvalīs in Lévi's *Nepal*, ii. 131-132; Kirkpatrick, 261-262.

[3] Only the Third Ṭhākurī Dynasty—I.A., IX, 414—6 names—Jayachandra Malla to Aśoka Malla coming before Jayasthiti Malla (1380-1354 A.D.), never ruled and are to be excluded. They must have been subordinate rulers.

manuscripts of Nepal (*Cat.*, p. 21ff). It is therefore not necessary for me to deal with the list after Rāghavadeva (880 A. D.). The names from Rāghavadeva to the end of the dynasty in the Vaṁśāvalī cited by Bendall (14th century) are:

Rāghavadeva 880 A.D. (46 yrs. 6 months)
Jayadeva (III) (10 yrs.)
Vikramadeva (8 yrs. 9 months)
Narendradeva (III) (1 yr. 6 months)
Guṇakāmadeva (II) (65 yrs. 5 months)
Udayadeva II (1018[1] A.D., according to the total of the above reign-period; (5 yrs. 5 months)
Nirbhaya (MS., 1008; A.D.) (K., 7 yrs.)

Joint rule:
- Bhojadeva (dated MS., 1015 A.D., not in Bendall's V. list)
- [Rudra not in any V.]
- Lakshmīkāmadeva (1015 A.D., dated manuscript) (21 yrs.)

Jayakāmadeva, 1039 A.D., MS., 'reign over half the kingdom' (20 yrs.) (Bendall's V.; at first joined with the two above).

Against this we have in the other lists :

[Rāghavadeva, only in K., 63 yrs.].
12 Jayadeva (III) (15 yrs.)
13 Balārjunadeva (17 yrs.) [in K. he is above Rāghavadeva]
14 Vikramadeva (12 yrs.)
[Narendradeva, only in K., 1½ yrs.]
15 Guṇakāmadeva (II) (51 yrs.)

[1] There must be a mistake of at least 10 yrs. because the next king's date is 1008 A.D. (Bendall, p. 21).

[Udaya, only in K., 6 yrs.]
[Nirbhaya, only in K., 7 yrs.]
16 Bhojadeva (8 yrs.)
17 Lakshmīkāmadeva (22 yrs.)

In the latter list no. 13 Balārjunadeva is extra. But in the list of Kirkpatrick's Vaṁśāvalī, which is in age next to Bendall's and earlier than Wright's and Bhagwanlal's, we have Balārjuna above Rāghavadeva who is omitted by other Vaṁśāvalīs. Hence the correct order seems to be that Balārjunadeva should come before Rāghavadeva[1], i.e.

[12] Balārjunadeva
Rāghavadeva
[13] Jayadeva III etc.

The succession of the Ṭhākurī line before Rāghavadeva, thus corrected, stands in the following order. [Fortunately at this period we begin to get reliable reign-periods. The Vaṁśāvalīs place these below Aṁśuvarman, 42 yrs., K., but they come really below Śivadeva II, as Aṁśuvarman is misplaced from below Śivadeva I to below Śivadeva II; and Jayadeva II (son of Śivadeva II) is omitted. Then the order runs thus :]

(2) Kṛitavarman [18 yrs. (K.), 654 A.D.[2]]
(3) Bhīmārjunadeva I [39 yrs. (K.), 672 A.D.]
(4) Nandadeva 'introduced the Era of Śālivāhana in Nepal' [13 yrs. (K.), 711 A.D.]

[1] In K. the names Balārjuna and Jayadeva have been repeated three times—evidently the composer who was consulting three authorities copied three orders. All this confusion is cleared up by Bendall's authority.

[2] Dates are calculated back from 880 A.D. for Rāghavadeva (see above).

(5) Śivadeva II (K.) 16 yrs., 724 A.D.
[Vîradeva—other recensions]

(6) Chandraketudeva, [omitted by K., did not complete even a year according to others] 740 A.D.

(7) Narendradeva [instituted Tibetan Buddhist worship, and several foundations] 37 yrs. (K.), 7 yrs. (W.) 740—777 A. D.

(8) Varadeva, 17 yrs. (K.), 23 yrs. (L.) 8 yrs. (W.) 777-784 A.D.

(9) Śaṁkaradeva 12 yrs. (all authorities) 784-796 A.D.

(10) Vardhamānadeva 13 yrs., 16 yrs., (K.) (Bhīmārjunadeva (K.) 812 A.D.

(11) Balideva 13 yrs., 16 yrs. (K.) 828 A.D.

(12) Balārjunadeva 36 yrs., (36 yrs., 7ms. (K.), other 17 yrs.) 844 A. D.

Rāghavadeva 46 yrs. (Bendall) 880-926 A.D.

It seems that Kṛitavarman and Bhīmārjunadeva I did not reign; no reign period is given to them by Wright's Vaṁśāvalī, nor is any event ascribed to them. They are mere names. They might have been feudatories, or only ancestors introduced here to give a complete genealogy from Aṁśuvarman. Their reign-periods given in Bhagwanlal's and Lévi's Vaṁśāvalīs—87 and 93 years—attempt to bridge the time roughly between Aṁśuvarman and Sivadeva II. The alternative years for them in Kirkpatrick's Vaṁśāvalī (18 and 39) will make their branch begin about *c* 654 A.D.

The line should be counted from No. 5 Sivadeva II, the three names before are probably of feudatories. The descent seems to have been thus :

Aṁśuvarman

- Udayadeva
  - Narendradeva I 643-657 A.D. [Chinese History]
    - Sivadeva II 714 A.D. (inscription) 724-740 (Vaṁśāvalī)
- Mānadeva II 639 or 640 A.D. [inscription]
- Kṛitavarman 654-672 (Vaṁ. date)
  - Bhīmārjunadeva I 672-711 (Vam. date)
    - Nandadeva 711-724 (Vaṁśāvalī date)

Sivadeva II and Nandadeva:

- Jayadeva II 748 A.D. (insc.) [omitted in *Vaṁ.*]
- Chandraketudeva 740 (Vaṁśāvalī date)
  - Narendradeva II 740-777 (Vaṁśāvalī date)
    - Varadeva 777-784 (Vaṁśāvalī date)
      - Nos. 9 to 13 (Rāghavadeva) 880[1] (Vaṁśāvalī date)

The omission of Jayadeva II by the Vaṁśāvalīs in both lists—Lichchhavi and Ṭhākurī—is significant. After Sivadeva II the main authority seems to have passed to Chandraketudeva whose

[1] Kirkpatrick, p. 202.

succession is noted to have been disputed, evidently, by Jayadeva II who is not given the full title of sovereignty in his inscription. Probably Chandraketudeva was the elder, and Jayadeva II a usurper. Sivadeva II is given both in the Lichchhavi line (no. 27) after Udayadeva and Mānadeva (with the misplaced Guṇakāmadeva) and in the Ṭhākurī line. This confusion resulted in the Chroniclers because they had read the inscription of Jayadeva II, and on account of the claim of the descendants of Aṁśuvarman to be the true Lichchhavi heirs[1]. But the chronology adopted by the Vaṁśāvalīs[2] is correct and agrees with the inscriptional dates and dates from Chinese History. The Ṭhākurī list further proves by the repetition of Sīvadeva II that the line of Udayadeva really descended from Aṁśuvarman.

Defeat of Jayāpīḍa Vinayāditya (782—813 A.D.) *of Kashmir by Nepal*

Jayāpīḍa, the Karkoṭa king of Kāśmir, whose history is related at length by Kalhaṇa in his History of Kāshmir, c. iv, verses 402-659, came to throne 48½ years after the accession of Muktāpīḍa Lalitāditya who had been invested by the Emperor of China in 733 A.D. He therefore became king in or about 782 A.D. and ruled for

[1] One *Vaṁśāvalī* cited in Mr. Landon's book *Nepal*, ii, 315 (Baḍā Kaji's Vaṁśāvalī) says that Aṁśuvarman had been adopted as son by Śivadeva I.

[2] That is, the chronology based on the date 880 A.D. for the beginning of the reign of Rāghavadeva, founder of the Nepal Era.

31 years, up to 813 A.D. He is related to have minted an unprecedented quantity of copper dinnāras (verse 617) which is attested by "multitudes" of his coins surviving today.[1] Jayāpīḍa distinguished himself both as king and scholar. He had great daring and desired to be Emperor of India. His exploits extended from the plains of Hindustan to Nepal. He was utterly defeated by the able tactics, peculiarly Nepalese, of the king of Nepal, and was taken prisoner. He was confined in a high stone-tower over the Kāla Gaṇḍikā (modern *Kāli Gaṇḍak*) until rescued by his faithful minister Devaśarman who pursuaded the Nepal king to promise to release him for a ransom, and obtained an interview with his master on that pretext. This episode has been unnecessarily disbelieved by V. Smith (p. 387). The very details and circumstantial and internal evidence furnished by Kalhaṇa affirm the truth of the account. It should be remembered that it was recent history in the time of Kalhaṇa who wrote his History in 1148-1150 A.D. The account runs as follows :

Jayāpīḍa started on a *dig-vijaya* with a large cavalry and reached Prayāga (413-417). After establishing his influence by his marriage at Puṇḍravardhana where he went secretly, he defeated the king of Kānyakubja with the help of Bengal and carried away his imperial Lion (*siṁhāsana*) Throne (471) and returned to Kashmir after three years, where he was welcomed by his people, who were keen to suppress his traitorous minister Jajja. He made Udbhaṭa, a man of letters, President of his Council, and the famous Dāmodaragupta, author of the *Kuṭṭanīmata*, his chief minister. He put up buildings, made reforms,

[1] V. Smith, EH, 387.

blished a 'Moving Bank' to follow his army, and assumed the name *Vinayāditya* (517).

He went as a spy into the eastern kingdom of Bhīmasena, evidently on his border, and was taken prisoner, from which condition he escaped simulating a contagious disease. On his release he invaded the neighbouring kingdom of Nepal, which was under King Aramuḍi.

King Aramuḍi, endowed with the art of war and valour, a skilled tactician, planned Jayāpīḍa's defeat (verse 531). He allowed Jayāpīḍa to enter the kingdom and retreated to 'a great distance' with his army, occasionally making himself visible to the pursuing Jayāpīḍa (533-34) who all the time imagined on account of his success in small encounters during the pursuit that he was having a victorious march. J. planted himself on the bank of a river near a large lake, to the east, when on the second or the third day he found to his 'indignation' the enemy facing him with his colours on the other side of the river. The enraged Jayāpīḍa ordered his army to cross the river which was only knee-deep. [The Nepalese knew their terrain and knew the use of their rivers]. The Kashmir army and their king were swept down by the current which suddenly rose and became irresistible. Cries arose from the bed of the river of distress and that of joy from the opposite bank. Aramuḍi promptly had Jayāpīḍa caught at a great distance down the river by the alert Nepalese soldiers with the aid of skins and brought before him with his fine clothes and ornaments of royalty having been deprived by the river. The occasion was celebrated by the Nepalese. He was assigned to a tall tower of stone on the river *Kāla Gaṇḍikā* [the river now called Kālī Gaṇḍak in western Nepal] where he was very closely guarded by the trusted men of the '*wise king*' of Nepal (546-548). Kalhaṇa notes that ślokas composed by the king Jayāpīḍa in that confinement, looking down upon the free river, were recited by learned men with pathos even in his own days (550).

Then follows the proposal to king Aramuḍi by the

Kashmir minister to release Jayāpīḍa on receiving a ransom and on condition to make Kashmir a dependency of Nepal. Devaśarman received permission to meet his master Jayāpīḍa, and affected his escape by ultimately committing suicide and thereby offering his body as a float.

This latter detail may be an exaggeration of an accident in the attempt of the minister to swim across the river with his master. But the rest of the account is a matter of fact narration recorded by Kashmir at the cost of her own reputation—a statement against her own interest.

Prof. Lévi not recognising the name in the Vaṁśāvalīs, declared with his Tibetan bias, the king called *Aramuḍi* to be a Tibetan. But Kāshmîrîs knew the Tibetans too well to make a mistake like that. *Kāla Gaṇḍikā*, still called *Kālī Gaṇḍak* and the western portion of Nepal where the scene is located offer verification of the story.

In the Nepal Vaṁśāvalīs we have four steps above Rāghavadeva, founder of the Nepal Era of 880 A.D. (Bendall, *Nepal Catalogue*, p. 21; I.A, IX, 413) *Vara-deva*[1]. *Vara-deva* or 'King *Vara*', (771-784 A.D.)[2] suits the chronology to be a contemporary of Jayāpīḍa (782-813 A.D.). *Vara* seems to have changed into *Ara*. Varadeva ruled a second

[1]Varadeva
Śaṅkaradeva
Vardhamānadeva
Balideva
[Rāghavadeva]
Jayadeva

The chronology from Rāghavadeva downwards is fully detailed and made certain by Dr. Bendall.

[2] See above the preceding part of this section.

time, having entered a monastery as a Buddhist monk (Wright, 142).[1] Or, *Ara* [in Kāshmîrî meaning hair (Grierson, *Dictionary*, p. 41)] and *muḍi* (*muṇḍita*) might denote '*monk*' king.

There seems to be in the Vaṁśāvalīs, which are a record of superstitious Buddhist priests interested in glorification of Tāntrika gods and goddesses and their idols, the historical account as degenerated into a fantastic story. *Karkoṭa* is the name of the dynasty to which Jayāpīḍa belonged. It is also the name of a famous Nāga worshipped in Kashmir and elsewhere in India. The Vaṁśāvalīs note that Gorakh-nath, the saint, arrived in Nepal in the reign of Varadeva and arrested Karkoṭa Nāga and imprisoned him in a hillock (Wright, pp. 140, 143). This caused a great mischief resulting in a draught. Then king Varadeva sought the help of Āchārya Bandhudatta who rescued and released Karkoṭa and established happiness in the valley. Bandhudatta had the pleasure of crossing rivers on the body of Karkoṭa all the same.

Fortunately the History of Kashmir has preserved this account which illustrates the successful traditional tactics of Nepal. Throughout the historian of Kashmir has used words of high respect for the Nepal king who defeated the idol of Kāshmir history—a most courageous figure, a most able king, an accomplished scholar, their greatest patron of men of letters and of letters—although his last days were marked with disregard for temple property which he largely

[1] This will fall after 784 A. D.

resumed, and contempt for the Brahmin caste, yet he remained a figure of whom Kashmir has been proud.

There is no reason to transfer from Nepal this chapter of glory to Tibet or to the domain of romance, as done by Lévi and Smith.

XII—Pala's connexion with Nepal and Nepal's later coinage

In the last quarter of the eighth century, that is, in the period after Jayadeva II, the Pāla Paramountcy begins in India, which remained on the increase in the reign of Dharmapāla (*c.* 800) and Devapāla (*c.* 850 A. D.) whose paramountcy did reach the Himalayan hill states (Kīra) and their borders (Assam). The Pāla emperors came in conflict with a Himalayan people called the Kāmbojas who broke the Pāla power for a time and who actually set themselves up at Dinajpur, where one of the routes from Nepal leads down to. This eclipse of the Pālas falls to be in the epoch when Nepal starts her own era in 880 A. D. Under Mahīpāla I the Pāla empire recovered (about 978 or 980).[1] During his reign Buddhism in Tibet was revived by new missions from Bihar, and we take it that Nepal was not ignored. Naya Pāla, his successor, who defeated Karṇa Kalachuri was succeeded by a wicked and weak son, Mahī Pāla II, who was succeeded by the powerful Rāma Pāla (1084-1130). His rule covered Mithilā and Assam (V. Smith, E. H., 416). We have positive evidence, which had been

[1] V. Smith, E. H., pp. 414-415.

missed so far, that R ā m a P ā l a was the suzerain of Nepal also.

A palm-leaf manuscript—*Kubjikāmatam* which is a part of the Tāntrika Buddhist work *Kulālikāmnāya* is in the Nepal State Library (H. P. Sastri, Catalogue, p. 54) which is in Newārī characters. It notes in the colophon that the manuscript was copied under the reign of the Buddhist Emperor R ā m a p ā l a d e v a:

Parameśvara-Parama-bhaṭṭāraka
parama-Saugata-Mahārājādhirāja
Śrīmad-Rāmapāladevasya
pravardha—(i.e. pravardhamāna-vijaya-rājye).

The portion in front of *parameśvara* is read as *Rāmadevasya* which if it refers to the Nepal king has to be read as *Vāmadevasya* whose time as ascertained from manuscripts of his reign and his predecessor and successor is between 1077 and 1090 A. D. (Bendall, Nepal Catalogue, *Intro*. p. 22).

We have thus positive proof of the fact that at least in the time of R ā m a P ā l a Nepal was under Pāla suzerainty. It is very likely that under D h a r m a P ā l a and D e v a P a l a a similar state obtained.

We do not find Nepal striking her own coins from about 800 A. D. onwards. This is probably explained by the fact of the Pāla domination, which was immediately followed by the K ā r n ā ṭ a k a domination beginning with N ā n y a d e v a. At the close of the K ā r n ā ṭ a k a period we find Nepal imitating the coin of Alauddin Khilji.[1] Then follows a troubled period until stability is restored under

[1] See separate article on the Unrecorded Muhammadan Invasion of Nepal in JBORS., XXII. 81.

Jayasithimalla[1] (1380-1394). Nepal acknowledged nominal suzerainty of Delhi as noted by Travernier.[2] And naturally we do not find a Nepal coinage until permission for establishing a mint was obtained from the early Moghuls.

Nepal thus from 800 A. D. or at any rate from 1080 A. D. remained as part of the Indian Empire up to Moghul days in international theory, which found a tangible expression in the history of her coinage—the absence of coinage. The same is to be predicated of her in the Imperial Gupta times as well.

B

EARLY DYNASTIES OF NEPAL

XIII—"NIMISHA DYNASTY" [205 A.D. TO 350 A.D.] AND KIRATA DYNASTY [590 B.C. TO 110 A.D.]

The Vaṁśāvalīs[3] other than Kirkpatrick's give five names at the close of the native Kirāta Dynasty and before the Sūryavaṁśa, i.e., the Lichchhavi Dynasty of Nepal—*Nimisha* (*Nevesit*—K.)—*Manāksha* (or *Matāksha*), *Kāka-varman*, *Paśupreksha-deva* (founder of the Paśupati Temple who introduced Aryan population from Hindustan) and *Bhāskara-varman* (who conquered the whole of India, and being childless adopted *Bhūmivarman*). They call this

[1] There was a Khasiyā invasion (1328 A. D.—Bendall, p. 10) and to that period must belong the curious clay coins of *Mathi singha Khasiyā*. The legend, in Nāgarī, is on the milled edge.

[2] II. ch. XV.

[3] Bhagwanlal Indraji's recension summarised in I. A., XIII. 411 at 412; Wright's copy in his *History of Nepal*, 112; Lévi's copy summarised in his *Nepal*, ii. 83.

Somavaṁśī dynasty. With *Bhūmivarman* whose grandson was Jayadeva I (mentioned in the inscription of Jayadeva II) the later Vaṁśāvalīs begin a new dynasty (the Sūryavaṁśa). But Kirkpatrick's authority while mentioning this adoption, does not begin a new dynasty and treats the two groups as forming one dynasty 'Nevesit'. It begins the dynasty with *Nevesit.* This *Nevesit* is really *Nevesi* corresponding with *Nimisha* of the later works, which have really turned **Nivisi* into *Nimisha.* '*Nivisi*' represented **Nichivi* (**Nisivi*) = *Nichchhivi* (Manu)= *Lichchhavi.* There was no distinct dynasty of a Somavaṁśa of the five rulers in the original authorities.

The seven rulers before Jayadeva I were rulers obviously in the plains, that is, at Vaiśālī. They annexed Nepal about 200 A. D. and established a direct government there, marking the event with the installation of Paśupati—which is a Mukhaliṅga of the style of the Nāga-Vākāṭakas, i.e., of the period.[1] '*Nimisha*' being only the dynastic name the first ruler of Nepal would be Mānāksha or Matāksha, and the effective founder, Paśuprekha the third king, who is credited with the introduction of Hindu caste-rules and population (of four varṇas) from Hindustan, and as being the founder of Paśupati's Temple.

His successor Bhāskaravarman, the great conqueror of India, is probably the grandfather of Samudra Gupta, and father-in-law of Chandragupta I. He was still probably the President

[1] See my *History of India,* 150-350 A. D., the plates and description of the Nachnā and other images.

of the Republic at Vaiśālī, for the coins of Chandra Gupta I are struck by the "*Lichchhavis.*" He seems to have defeated Magadha and evidently his dominions were large enough to entitle Chandra Gupta I to call himself *Mahārājādhirāja.* The seat of government changed from Vaiśālī to Nepal where his adopted son Bhūmivarman succeeded and the plains passed on to Chandra Gup-ta I and his Queen, the Lichchhavi lady. In Nepal Jayadeva I turned the state into a monarchy or a double kingship.

The succession seems to have stood thus:

Bhāskara-Varmā [or,-Deva]
|
Daughter=Chandra Gupta I
Bhūmi-Varmā (or,-Deva)
|
Jayadeva I

We may roughly date the Early Lichchhavis:

C. 205 A. D.	Mānāksha
C. 230 A.D.	Kāka-varman
C. 255 A. D.	Paśuprekshadeva
C. 280-305 A. D.	Bhāskaravarman
C. 305 A. D.	Bhūmivarman
C. 330 A. D.	Chandravarman [Is he the same as Chandra-Gupta I?]
C. 340 or 350 A. D.	Jayadeva I[1]

The Lichchhavi monarchy in Nepal probably retained its original character of divided sovereignty,

[1] This date is calculated on the basis of Jayadeva II's inscription: See Fleet, GI, *I.* p. 189; and other data in the section on Lichchhavi list, *supra.*

otherwise the position of Aṁśuvarman's dictatorship and Śivadeva's sovereignty is not explicable. Probably even before Aṁśuvarman some similar arrangement obtained.

Nimisha is said to have displaced the Kirāta Dynasty in Nepal—(205 A.D.).

The original Kirāta Dynasty which is the first dynasty of Nepal had 28 kings.[1] It was under the 15th Kirāta—Sthunko—that Aśoka visited Nepal. According to the Nepal Chronicles the autonomy of Nepal was maintained by Aśoka under the Kirāta dynasty. This may or may not be correct, as Aśoka's son-in-law Devapāla and his daughter became permanent residents there. After Aśoka and Daśaratha the original dynasty would have revived in Nepal Proper. In the Western part of Nepal in Śuṅga times we find silver coins of Śuṅga princes (Sumitra)[2], Imperial and local (Śivapālita). It is possible that early Śuṅgas might have exercised suzerainty over Nepal. But the continuous line of the Kirāta House entitles us to assume a continuous autonomy. The succession of 15 kings from the time of Aśoka and Sthunko would bring the dynasty to about 110 A. D. [see below].

We have thus a gap between the Kirāta and the Lichchhavi epochs—110 A. D. and 205 A. D.

[1] The Gupta and Ahīr dynasties introduced before the Kirātas (600 B. C.-110 A. D.) who are treated again with the kings of the Sixth and Seventh centuries A.D. are really misplaced here; it simply signifies that Hindu history in Nepal begins with the Gupta Period.

[2] Almora coins of alloyed silver; JBORS, XX. 301.

—which is not filled up by the written history of Nepal.

Here coins come to our help. Mr. E. H. Walsh has recorded (JRAS., 1908, p. 677) that a hoard of Kushan coins was dug up in the neighbourhood of Kāṭhmāṇḍu. They were coins of Wema Kadphises and of Kanishka. It seems that the Kushan rule might fill this gap of hundred years. Though evidence is not yet conclusive.

The beginning of the Kirāta dynasty (13 generations before Aśoka) is to be dated about 600 B. C.

The Kirāta Kings

Omitting *Yalamva* and *Pavi* [omitted in K.], as belonging to the Second Kirāta dynasty of the sixth century (§ VII), the approximate dates of the kings of the First Kirāta Dynasty will be as calculated below on the basis of the date of Sthunko, contemporary of Aśoka :

2.	Dhaskam	c. 590 B.C.
3.	Valamva	c. 565 B.C.
4.	Hṛiti	c. 540 B.C.
5.	Humati	c. 515 B.C.
6.	[Tuskhah] K.	c. 490 B.C.
7.	Jitedāsti [Sroopast-K.]	c. 465 B.C.
8.	[Galiṁja]	c. 440 B.C.
9.	P (T)ushka Paṃcham (K.)	c. 415 B.C.
10.	Suyarma [King-king-king (K.)]	c. 390 B.C.
11.	Parba [Soonand-K.]	c. 365 B.C.
12.	Thuṅka [Thoomoo-K.]	c. 340 B.C.
13.	Keṁke	c. 315 B.C.
14.	Svananda [Jaighree-K.]	c. 290 B.C.
15.	Sthuṁko [contemporary of Aśoka] ..	c. 265 B.C.
16.	Gighri [Suenkeh-K.]	c. 240 B.C.

17.	Nane [Thoor-K.]	..	..	.. c. 215 B.C.
18.	Luk [Thamoo-K.]	..	..	.. c. 190 B.C.
19.	Thor [Barmah-K.]	..	..	.. c. 165 B.C.
20.	Thoko [Ganjeh-K.]	..	..	.. c. 140 B.C.
21.	Varma [Kashkoon-K.]		..	.. c. 115 B.C.
22.	Guja [Teeshoo-K.]	..	..	.. c. 90 B.C.
23.	Pushka [Soogmeea-K.]		..	.. c. 65 B.C.
24.	Kesu [Joosha-K,]	..	..	.. c. 40 B.C.
25.	Suga [Gontho-K.]	..	..	.. c. 15 B.C.
26.	Sansa [Khembhoom-K.]		..	.. c. 10 A.D.
27.	Gunan [Galijang-K.]	..	..	.. c. 35 A.D.
28.	Khimbu	..	..	.. c. 60 A.D.
29.	Paṭuka	..	..	.. c. 85 A.D.
30.	Gasti	..	..	.. c. 110 A.D.

It may be noted that the popular tradition in Nepal today is that the first dynasty of Nepal was *Kirātī*, second *Newārī*, and lastly *Gorkhā*.

C

A RETROSPECT

XIV

The history of Nepal is a part of the history of India and of the Hindu Race. The valley was colonized by the Hindus both consciously and by natural process of expansion. Yet it is the history of a colony, with its distinctive features. Those features may be summarised in this way. The ruling dynasties, though mostly Hindus from the plains of India—the Mauryas, the Lichchhavis, the Kārnāṭakas, the Gorkhas—have a tendency to establish a system of divided sovereignty which works happily in that happy valley of Paśupati. There is much less cause for jealousy in that system on the soil of Nepal than anywhere else. Joint rules and regencies are a familiar problem in the Lichchhavi times, in the Ṭhākurî times, in the Malla times and in the Gurkha times—two kings occupying the same town or contiguous towns afford a picture of a Mitāksharā family agreeing upon, as we say in Hindu law, a 'division for the convenience of enjoyment' rather than upon an actual division by metes and bounds. This divided sovereignty would baffle theorists of political science but has been a familiar, good working system in Nepal.

There is always a sort of internal weakness, but to the outside world Nepal has always shown strength. Throughout her history there has been no case of traitorous betrayal. Internally weak, but externally strong is again a political problem which is explainable by its republican origin noticed above. Nepal's whole history bears out the rule that the little kingdom can defend itself most effectively—it defeated Tibet in her palmiest days when Tibet was the first power in Asia, it defeated Kashmir when Kashmir was the first power in India, it defeated King Shamsuddin, the most brilliant Muslim soldier of the 14th century. Small, and 'internally weak,' Nepal is a successful state against the invader. And why? Its republican Lichchhavi origin explains the mystery. Its strong political sense is a Lichchhavi heritage.

Nepal has been in Hindu times mostly a member of the Indian Empire. But for centuries, being situated between two large empires—China and India—Nepal has evolved a wise international policy, wherein she has hardly ever taken a false step. Owing to that wise policy, her international position today is such as it had probably never been before. She enjoys and rightly the complete confidence of her powerful neighbour.

INDEX

A

C

H

I

U

V